CONGRESS

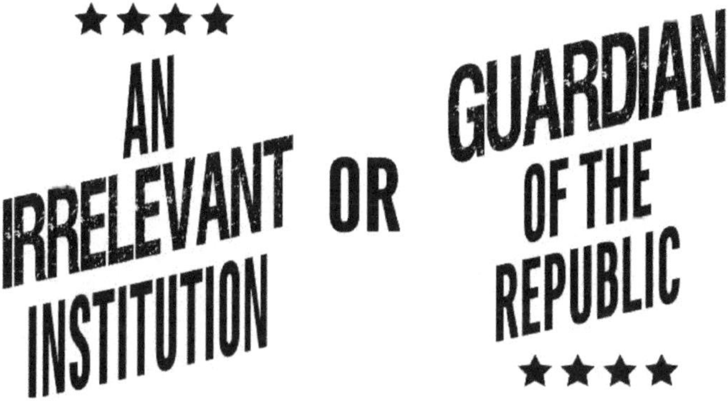

William L. Kovacs

Publishing Coordinator & Book Designer – Sharon Kizziah-Holmes

Paperback-Press
an imprint of Paperback Press, LLC
Springfield, Missouri

ISBN -13: 978-1-970560-23-7

ACKNOWLEDGMENT OF POLITICAL REALITY

Congress has reached a fork in the road. If its members continue their current path of loyalty to Presidents and political parties, they will lead the nation toward authoritarianism. If members take the path of loyalty to the Constitution by serving as fiduciaries to the institution of Congress and defending the separation of powers, they will preserve the Republic.

CONTENTS

Acknowledgment of Political Reality
Introduction
Part 1 Future Political Shock Post – 2029
Chapter 1
The Ghost of Politics Yet to Come 1
Chapter 2
The Opportunity Party's First Actions 6
Part II Congress Makes Itself Irrelevant 20
Chapter 3
Congress Created a Subsidy Society 21
Chapter 4
The National Debt: An Egregious Breach of Fiduciary Duty 32
Chapter 5
Congress Fiddles While Presidents Burn the Constitution 39
Chapter 6
National Emergencies: Congress Builds the Road to Dictatorship 43
Chapter 7
The President's Hostile Takeover of Congress by Executive Orders 51
Chapter 8
From Regulatory Sclerosis to State Capitalism............ 57
Chapter 9
How the Courts and Administrative State Maneuvered Congress 64
Part III Serving as a Fiduciary in Congress 74
Chapter 10
Legislating Is Only a Fiduciary Power 75
Chapter 11
Examples of Fiduciary Courage that Changed Nations 84

Part IV Creating an Accountable Government............ 90
Chapter 12
Only Congress Can Create an Accountable Government 91
Chapter 13
Accountability and Fairness Begin by Simplifying Taxes 97
Chapter 14
Accountability Requires Substantially Reducing the National Debt 104
Chapter 15
Truth as the First Duty of Government 113
Chapter 16
Congress Should Never Delegate Declaring War 124
Chapter 17
Congress Must Deploy Its Anti-Takeover Defenses... 131
Chapter 18
A Candidate's Fiduciary Pledge to Preserve the Republic 138
Part V Congress Must Write the Ending 140
Chapter 19
The Ghost of Politics Yet to Come Is Still in the Room 141
Postscript 146
About the Author 150

INTRODUCTION

Congress: An Irrelevant Institution or Guardian of the Republic describes a nation standing at the edge of a gathering storm. In Washington's marble halls, the slow, almost imperceptible transfer of power from Congress to the presidency has become a silent revolution. No tanks roll. No proclamations announce a new regime. The Constitution remains as written. Yet the shift is real, building with every crisis declared, every executive order issued, and every presidential overreach Congress refuses to resist. The central question now confronting the nation is chilling in its simplicity: Will Congress rise to defend the Constitution, or will it allow the presidency to exercise powers our founders never intended it to possess?

While the future of the United States remains unwritten, Congress's actions are very troubling for the Republic. Each failure to check executive ambition erases a boundary the founders drew in blood and conviction. What replaces those boundaries appears to be an executive that rules by impulse rather than deliberation, by command rather than law. If Congress allows this gradual erosion to continue, America will simply drift into the very form of concentrated power the framers feared most.

Congress alone holds the power to stop that slide. But should Congress refuse to shoulder its duties, the responsibility will fall to the people themselves, the ultimate guardians of the Republic. The fate of constitutional government now hinges on whether Congress and the people will act before the point of no return.

This book explores the consequences when members of Congress prioritize the demands of a president, who is the leader of their political party, over the Constitution that mandates they restrain presidential power. Although it was written during the first year, 2025, of the second Trump presidency, its premise transcends administrations. Every president seeks to expand executive power. Every Congress that prioritizes party over principle aids this expansion by eroding the separation of powers. The only difference between Democrat and Republican presidents is their methods of using power and their targets. Some wield power with brutal force, others with deceptive bureaucratic finesse—but the outcome is the same: a government moving away from consent to central rule.

Each new president inherits not only the office, but also the precedent of unchecked authority acquired by predecessors. That accumulation of presidential power has made Congress nearly irrelevant. President Trump treats a compliant Congress as an extension of his staff—defending his right to dictate policy and law alike. With the near-unanimous backing of his party, he governs through intimidation: punishing dissent, withholding funds, weaponizing enforcement, and threatening those who resist, from the press to the courts. His attempt to merge personal and public powers under the banner of protecting "freedom" and "national security" marks a dangerous turning point toward centralized control of the nation.

President Biden sought to wield power as much as Trump, though with less threatening rhetoric. He issued unconstitutional executive orders—canceling student debt, mandating vaccinations, ignoring immigration law—while his party in Congress looked away. Like Trump, he treated the Constitution not as the foundation of policy, but as a hindrance to it. The cumulative effect is the same: an executive branch ruling by decree while Congress stands by, watching its own authority evaporate.

This erosion of constitutional balance did not begin with either man. Since the Gulf of Tonkin Resolution, Congress has repeatedly abandoned its role—allowing presidents from

Johnson to Trump to wage wars, spend trillions, and govern without debate. The failure is not merely personal; it is institutional. When Congress becomes an arm of the president rather than the people's branch, it ceases to function as a check on power and instead becomes the mechanism that enhances presidential power.

Congress is the only branch elected directly by the people. It is the only institution citizens can directly approach for redress. When it honors its constitutional duty, the people are protected by law. When it serves only partisan interests, the people are protected only by the political party in power. Each time Congress submits to presidential rule, it abandons its fiduciary duty of loyalty to the institution of Congress and the very idea of a government limited by consent.

That abandonment of fiduciary duty is the center point of the book. The hope is to instill in members of Congress the fundamental need to serve as fiduciaries, giving their loyalty to Congress and the Constitution, not the president, political party, or supporters.

Rather than begin with a list of lost powers, Part I, "Future Political Shock Post-2029," opens by describing the road ahead, a vision of our near future: a United States that looks familiar, yet eerily foreign. The Constitution still exists, elections are held, and courts still issue opinions—but the nation has lost its vibrancy. It is sadly expressionless. The president rules not as one branch among three, but as commander-in-chief of them all. Congress still convenes, but its debates are theater. The judiciary still issues opinions, but they have so little impact that they may have been written with invisible ink.

The façade of democracy remains; the substance is gone. This is the destination toward which congressional inaction leads.

The road ahead.

The chapters that follow trace how this transformation took root—and, more importantly, how Congress can reclaim its constitutional role as Guardian of the Republic.

- Part II describes how Congress has made itself irrelevant by creating a subsidy society, accepting executive orders and emergency declarations as national policy, and acquiescing to being maneuvered into irrelevance by the Administrative State.
- Part III argues that every member of Congress is a trustee of the Constitution and owes a fiduciary duty of loyalty to the institution of Congress.
- Part IV presents clear, reasonable reforms that, if implemented, will make government accountable and give citizens reasons to trust it again.
- Part V returns to the road ahead and how Congress and citizens might preserve the Republic.

PART 1

FUTURE POLITICAL SHOCK POST – 2029

CHAPTER 1

THE GHOST OF POLITICS YET TO COME

We the People created this Union. It is our responsibility to keep it as faithful to the Constitution as possible. While its future is never written, we must all recognize that those seeking power over us must serve as trustees of the Constitution and fiduciaries to the institutions we elect them to; otherwise, they will use their power to dominate us.

How political power shifts occur.

The future of American politics is shaped by the choices we make at the ballot box, in our communities, and on the streets. Yet a new global pattern is emerging, and incumbent parties are increasingly punished for failing to satisfy voters. Around the world, ruling coalitions lose seats or popular support with each election cycle. This trend shows no sign of slowing—and its implications for democracy are profound.

If this "throw-the-bums-out" impulse persists, a U.S.

election soon could deliver overwhelming power to whichever party is out of office. The potential consequences of such a shift are significant, as the party may campaign on promises to uplift ordinary citizens, but once enthroned, its leaders often follow a familiar path, consolidating authority, rewarding allies, and settling old scores.

Because most members of Congress instinctively defend presidents of their own party, each administration accelerates the erosion of legislative power. The fictional scenario that follows in Chapter 2 is meant as a warning, but it reflects conversations long whispered in both major parties. No complete plan to seize permanent control has yet been developed—but the temptation to do so is ever-present. To see how such a shift could occur, we must first understand how presidential power accumulates over time.

The outcome will ultimately depend on the courage and integrity of Congress. To prevent a "Future Political Shock Post-2029," lawmakers must reclaim their constitutional role as an independent check on executive ambition. Only a legislature that enforces the separation of powers can ensure that the nation remains free. The balance of power must be restored—before it is too late.

It can happen here.

America may face an even more radical transformation if one party gains the presidency and commands large majorities in both chambers of Congress. Such dominance will likely follow the rule of an authoritarian president who failed to consolidate total control. In the next election, fearful voters might hand the opposition overwhelming power, trusting its pledge to "restore constitutional order."

Yet once in office, the new rulers could employ the same constitutionally sounding maneuvers as their predecessors while passing repressive laws at breakneck speed to entrench their authority. Every past power grab becomes a training manual for the next. Future would-be dictators will know precisely how far they can stretch the Constitution without generating universal opposition. And the next time the presidency, Congress, and a compliant Court align, the Republic will be left with no institutional brake strong enough to stop them.

How does this happen?

We now live in an era when presidents use the federal government to rule citizens rather than serve them. Congress, too often paralyzed by partisanship, chooses irrelevance over confrontation. Slowly—without altering a single word of the Constitution, the federal government shifts from servant to master.

Executive power has been expanding since the founding of the Republic, steadily absorbing authority once held by the states. Presidents now command vast bureaucracies and use their resources to encroach on Congress itself.

Presidents Biden and Trump exemplify this modern pattern. Each issued sweeping executive orders, declared national emergencies, selectively implemented or ignored laws, and directed agencies to pursue political objectives regardless of congressional intent. The "whole-of-government" model is the new norm. It requires every federal agency to advance all of the President's priorities, even when those priorities are unrelated to its mission. Policy reversals on diversity, climate, immigration, and government spending underscore the broad scope of executive discretion.

These reversals illustrate how presidents of both parties exploit the same statutes to advance opposite agendas. Consider Diversity, Equity, and Inclusion (DEI) mandates: President Biden issued them to protect the rights of minority groups. President Trump rescinded them and issued an order of the opposite effect, citing equal-protection principles under the very same laws.

Congress rarely intervenes in the realm of executive orders and emergency declarations. The executive branch no longer merely executes the law—it increasingly creates it. Each administration inherits and expands the powers of the last, edging the nation closer to authoritarian rule. Biden's 2021–2025 term reversed most of Trump's actions issued during his first term. Trump's 2024 platform promised total reversals of Biden's.

In Trump's second term (2025–2029), he is fulfilling those promises. Once reelected, he moved decisively, cutting budgets, dismantling departments he disfavored, firing civil servants by converting the federal workforce to "at-will" status, terminating programs, and issuing executive orders targeting law firms, universities, and corporations viewed as opponents.

Although lawsuits challenged these actions, the administration continued testing the limits of its constitutional power. Trump perceives himself, as will all future presidents, as untouchable after the Supreme Court granted broad immunity from criminal prosecution for official acts. He enforces laws by executive fiat, not by statutory enactment or judicial orders.

With a compliant Congress and a sympathetic Court, genuine checks on presidential excess have vanished. If a partisan majority shields a president from impeachment and conviction, the president is free to act with impunity. Without constitutional restraints, the presidency itself becomes a law unto itself.

The Opportunity Party emerges.

Each presidential reversal of established policy or constitutional norms, without congressional involvement, underscores the dwindling relevance of Congress and illustrates how presidents exploit executive power.

Red and blue states alike are now manipulating congressional districts to secure partisan advantage, shaping the future balance of Congress, and protecting presidents of their own party. The legislature becomes an accomplice in its own subjugation.

To his most devoted supporters, Trump is almost mythic, to his opponents, a corrupt strongman. Both perceptions expose the nation's deep divide. Democrats, meanwhile, study his methods as lessons they could one day employ. Once a tactic is normalized, every successor inherits its fruits.

Between 1899 and 2021, sixteen of twenty-one presidents governed with unified control of Congress—twelve of them Democrats. With legal immunity and congressional protection from impeachment, future administrations, regardless of party, will be tempted to govern through executive orders, routine emergency declarations, staff purges, and creative end-runs around judicial rulings. The pattern is clear: once acquired, executive power is rarely surrendered.

The only remaining check on an authoritarian presidency would be a Congress willing to act independently. Yet both parties appear eager to transform the United States into an executive-dominated state. The first party to succeed becomes the "Opportunity Party"—the pioneer of concentrated, constitutionalized power.

While fictional, the Opportunity Party is modeled on what could easily occur if Congress continues to abandon its constitutional duties. Examining Congress under Biden and Trump, one can envision a future Congress reduced to ceremony—obedient to the executive and lacking independent will.

In that government, the Opportunity Party treats norms as obstacles and laws as a weapon. What follows in Chapter 2 is not prophecy but plausible foresight: how an ambitious president might rule through executive decree, empowered by a compliant Congress and cheered by partisans who mistake domination for leadership.

CHAPTER 2

THE OPPORTUNITY PARTY'S FIRST ACTIONS

The federal government views citizens as mere commodities that pay taxes.

History teaches that government takeovers seldom begin with a bang. They unfold in slow motion. In the United States, the transformation has been hiding in plain sight for decades. Congress has been surrendering its powers, one quiet concession at a time, as presidents have been accumulating authority by simply picking it up off the floor. Eventually, the people's branch becomes a spectator, and the presidency evolves into something uncomfortably close to an elected monarchy. At that point, average citizens are afraid to ask their neighbors whether freedom still exists.

This chapter imagines the moment when that long decline of Congress meets presidential opportunity—a scenario entirely possible within the existing constitutional framework.

The times they are a-changing.

Sometime after 2029, the Opportunity Party wins 250 seats in the House and 57 in the Senate. It needs only three more senators to abolish the 60-vote cloture rule and end filibusters for good. For months, the Opportunity and Opposition party have attempted a grand bargain, but neither side has a political incentive to compromise. Budget battles trigger repeated shutdowns. The national debt reaches 200% of GDP. Artificial intelligence has displaced 40 percent of the workforce. The business sector still bows to presidential power in hopes of maintaining its subsidies. The economy staggers after the expulsion of most foreign university students, the very people who would have become the nation's next generation of scientists, engineers, and physicians.

Beyond America's borders, the world is shifting in ways the political class long dismissed as unlikely. The BRICS nations and their new partners adopt a competing reserve currency, weakening the U.S. ability to print dollars at will and sanction disfavored nations. China's military power surpasses that of the United States—a milestone reached after decades of denial. Most disturbingly, U.S. military bases abroad now face threats from advanced weapons systems manufactured in America and sold to our then allies by presidents seeking to create desperately needed jobs in the United States.

Beyond the point of no return.

Cooperation might rescue the nation, but neither Party seeks it. The Opportunity Party believes its numerical advantage justifies unilateral action. The Opposition Party sees obstruction as its only remaining relevance. Public dissatisfaction smolders, but mass protests are rare after decades of normalized domestic military presence have taught citizens where the unmovable lines rest. Surveillance is no longer a policy—it is an atmosphere.

Inside Congress, the President's grip is vise-like. Party members vote as instructed and are regularly reminded of what disobedience invites. Presidential punishment of party dissenters has transitioned from personal attacks and threats of primary challenges to promises of the release of the Federal Bureau of Investigation (FBI) files he has on them. Those members without files are well aware of a standing order to the Internal Revenue Service (IRS) to scrutinize their tax returns. Security agencies are encouraged to "look into" their families. The message is unmistakable: dissent has consequences.

The Opposition Party retains one weapon—the filibuster—and uses it to block transformative legislation. The president, convinced that history has granted him a narrow window, decides to crush the remaining obstacle.

Under pressure too intense to ignore, the president's congressional allies fall in line. The Opportunity Party prepares to act. It is fully aware that once it crushes the opposition, it will change the Republic forever. Once that first step is taken, the Opportunity Party knows it can never again allow an Opposition party to regain its voice, let alone govern.

The Opportunity Party acts.

1. The nuclear option.

Both parties have wanted to use the "nuclear option" for years to push their legislative agendas but have not out of fear of being on the receiving end of the punishment. Now, without a functioning Congress, the president demands that the Opportunity Party employ the nuclear option to repeal the Senate's filibuster rule in the name of "protecting the national security of the nation."

While Senate rules require only 51 votes to pass a bill, debate time is unlimited. To restrict debate, the Senate adopted Rule 22, which allows 60 members to invoke cloture—a procedure that ends debate and allows a vote. Any senator can object to ending debate, forcing the chamber to reach that 60-vote threshold. In a deeply divided Congress, this requirement has effectively paralyzed the Senate, preventing votes on more than two thousand bills.

An online magazine reported that only a decade ago, Senators filed 336 cloture motions to break filibusters. During the post-2029 period, nearly 1,000 cloture petitions were filed annually. Other than Rule 22 procedural motions, the Senate is inoperative.

Since Rule 22 is a Senate rule, not a law, the Senate can change it without House approval or the president's signature. Although changing the rule typically also requires 60 votes, there is an option the Opportunity Party could use to gain complete control of the chamber: the "nuclear option."

The nuclear option involves a series of procedural maneuvers that raise a point of order, prompt a ruling from the chair, and allow an appeal if that motion is denied. If the majority overrules the chair, a new precedent is established. When that precedent concerns the filibuster, debate on the affected matter can thereafter be closed by a simple majority vote.

Both major parties have already used the nuclear option to expedite the confirmation of presidential nominees, including judges and Supreme Court justices. The next logical step for the majority party is to eliminate the filibuster for all legislation.

The elimination of the filibuster and subsequent reforms could drastically reduce legislative oversight, enabling the Opportunity Party to implement policies that threaten civil liberties and democratic accountability.

Late one Thursday night, as the Senators were attempting to go home for the weekend the beginning of the end unfolds. The chamber was empty, except for C-Span cameras. The Majority Leader raised a procedural point of order. The scholarly parliamentarian denied the motion, ruling in favor of tradition. On cue, fifty-one senators quickly entered the chamber and voted to overturn the ruling. A new precedent was born—quietly, efficiently, and likely forever, the Senate would function like the House, by majority rule.

The next morning, a few cable channels reported the events as a "historic modernization." Talk-show hosts called it long overdue. The mainstream media was in a frenzy. Opposition Party Senators were on cable channels for hours, expressing their shock at the events. The president went on national television Friday afternoon to take full credit for restoring Democracy to the nation. The markets rallied massively, believing the federal government would now function. Eliminating the filibuster could mark the beginning of a new era, in which bills that had been stalled for years would move forward, and public opinion would overwhelmingly support the Senate's action.

By Tuesday, bills that had languished for years began sailing through. Public opinion was overwhelmingly in support of the Senate's action. Few appreciated that future political debate would be almost non-existent.

With the legislative logjam broken and the Opportunity Party firmly in control of Congress, it was time for the administration to take over the "rogue" judiciary once and for all.

2. Remaking the Supreme Court.

After watching past presidents restructure the federal government at will, the Opportunity Party is emboldened. With the filibuster gone, Congress can remake the Supreme Court to secure favorable rulings for its presidents for decades. The Constitution imposes no limit on the number of justices a president may appoint. An Opportunity Party-controlled Congress introduces legislation to increase the number of justices by ten. These new justices will ensure a reliable majority for decades.

Concurrently with the packing of the Supreme Court, fifty-two Opportunity Party Senators introduce legislation to reduce the number of lower court judges by fifty percent over the next decade.

On the floor of the Senate, a cosponsoring Senator explains:

> *The U.S. Supreme Court has not always consisted of nine justices. In the early 1800s, it was six. Between 1863 and 1866, there were ten. In the 1930s, President Franklin Roosevelt attempted to expand the Court to fifteen. Since the Constitution does not determine the number of justices, the Opportunity Party controlling Congress will select a number that would allow the current president to run the nation without interference from the opinions of a few second-tier lawyers masquerading as justices.*

By expanding the Supreme Court to 19 justices and reducing the number of judges on the lower courts, the Opportunity Party not only gains control over constitutional interpretation but also signals that judicial independence is conditioned on political loyalty. Once the Court becomes a political instrument rather than an arbiter of justice, the entire system of checks and balances tilts toward the ruling Party, which seeks to accumulate more power.

3. The prosperity illusion - Modern Monetary Theory, elimination of the debt ceiling.

The national debt, budget deficits, and the debt ceiling have plagued the nation since it reached its first trillion-dollar deficit in 1982. The president directed his economic team to devise a perfect solution. The president delivers an Oval Office address that reassures the country that it will emerge from its economic malaise in weeks. It will return to accelerated economic growth and create millions of jobs.

The following week, the president unveils the "National Liquidity Program" (NLP), an economic plan to ensure "continuity of fiscal operations, no matter the balance sheet of the nation." No one mentioned the economic philosophy that underpins the program: Modern Monetary Theory (MMT). Economists instead presented the idea as "monetary sovereignty" and "adaptive stabilization." The president assured the public that taxes would not rise. He called it a breakthrough in modern-day finance. The president claimed the new finance theory was worthy of a Nobel Prize in economics. With confidence—and likely support from a few members of the Opposition Party, the Opportunity Party next eliminates the statutory debt ceiling. This single act will free the government to borrow and spend whatever it deems necessary to maintain control. The Party's argument will be simple: the debt ceiling has never truly constrained spending since its creation in 1917.

The premise of the MMT is that a nation that controls its own currency can never go bankrupt. The central government owes its debts to itself, and new money can be created at no cost using a few computer keystrokes.

Under this theory, inflation is the only fundamental constraint. When prices rise, the government can raise taxes to cool down demand. If the central bank holds interest rates near zero, however, no meaningful debt repayment is ever required. New money is free.

While neither major Party ever proposed adopting MMT, in practice, both parties practiced it by running persistent deficits and manipulating interest rates to manage debt.

The result: money is created out of nothing, and hyperinflation is deemed "transitory." All will seem well—until it isn't. When the inevitable happens and faith in the currency collapses, the president will use the events to further solidify power. His Opportunity Party members in

Congress will give the president greater allegiance since they are his accomplices.

4. Creating new states.

The safest mechanism for entrenching power in the Opportunity Party is to create new states that favor the ruling Party.

If Democrats are the Opportunity Party, they will invoke Article IV, Section 3 of the Constitution to admit the District of Columbia and Puerto Rico as new states. That move would likely add two new Democratic House members and four Democratic Senators—enough to secure congressional control for decades.

If Republicans are the Opportunity Party, they will pursue a similar strategy by persuading Texas to divide into three states. Under its original terms of admission to the Union, Texas retained the right to divide itself into as many as five states, making such a maneuver constitutionally lawful. Since such a move would give the people of Texas far more representation and control over Congress than any other state, they are inclined to ratify the move. The Governor of Texas pledges to support the measure and works tirelessly to persuade the Governors' Association to do the same.

Congressional leadership promises to expedite the passage of legislation to implement the president's request. The Speaker of the House promises that if he cannot pass the measure, the House will initiate a process to form several new states within states that have legislatures willing to create them. The Speaker points to the division of Virginia into two states (West Virginia and Virginia) after the Civil War as support for its implementation.

5. Protecting voting rights.

Since the Constitution does not explicitly guarantee a federal right to vote, eligibility rules remain flexible.

A Democrat Opportunity Party would pledge to repeal the *1996 Illegal Immigration Reform and Immigrant Responsibility Act* to permit non-citizens to vote. It argues that the Fourteenth Amendment protects "persons," not only citizens. Following enactment, the Party could expect to increase its loyal voters by thirty percent through massive registration drives.

A Republican Opportunity Party would move in the opposite direction. It would restrict mail-in and early voting, tightening ID requirements, and shrinking the electorate to one more predictable. The Party chair argues, *The right to vote means only real votes count, those who can prove citizenship. That is the only way to protect a person's vote.*

In both cases, the Party defines Democracy to suit its power needs.

6. Reshaping the Electoral College.

Democrats, controlling several of the most populated states, want the direct election of the president. To accomplish this objective, the supporting states will seek to abolish or neutralize the Electoral College. Since a constitutional amendment is unlikely, they will champion the *National Popular Vote Interstate Compact* (the Compact), under which participating states agree to award all their electoral votes to the winner of the national popular vote. The Compact activates once states representing 270 electoral votes join. The Compact has eighteen states holding 209 votes signed on; seven more, representing 74 votes, are considering it.

Republicans, in response, will defend the Electoral College by manipulating the Census—counting only "well-documented Americans." These restrictions would reduce populations in large Democratic-leaning states like California, New York, and Illinois, lowering their congressional representation and electoral votes.

The fate of the Electoral College is key to retaining the presidency.

7. Governing through fear — the permanent emergency.

Regardless of which Party rules, both will find fear the most effective instrument of control. The new president will issue a series of emergency declarations covering the economy, communications, finance, transportation, civil order, and civil rights—effectively governing by decree. The rule of law will wither under the weight of perpetual emergency. Each declaration came with a sunset clause, always extended "until conditions normalize."

After observing the Trump presidency, both parties will likely become more comfortable deploying the National Guard and the military into domestic affairs. Troops walked the streets, but they were merely a political production. The real government intrusion into liberty will be unmarked drones patrolling demonstrations "for crowd safety," monitoring all data and voice communications to protect "children," and federal integration of security cameras, cell phones, and tags in all means of transportation, bags, shoes, clothing, and homes, to protect the general population. All television viewing is two-way and must be constantly on.

The judiciary will adapt to its new role. Lower courts will understand that their rulings carry no force if they restrain the executive. The Supreme Court recognizes that its survival depends on supporting the Opportunity Party. Lifetime appointments to the courts are rewards for loyalists rather than the implementation of the rule of law.

A copy of the Constitution hangs in every federal building. It just no longer governed the country.

8. The crown jewel — the third term is real.

The Twenty-Second Amendment bars anyone from being elected president more than twice. But in an era when political words bend before spines stiffen, the nation only operates in the field of uncertainty.

It begins solely with the dream of one person. The outgoing president, term-limited but still commanding his party, endorses his vice president as successor and handpicks a trusted ally as running mate. Their campaign promises "continuity of security." The public, content with low crime rates, accepts it.

Once elected, the new president appoints the former president as "Special Advisor to the Nation." The former president would serve as a consultant to the sitting president, without receiving a salary. His office will be next to the president's office, and he will be a daily presence in the Oval Office. The role would be like the one given to Elon Musk in the second Trump administration, who headed the Department of Government Efficiency (DOGE). Cabinet secretaries, unsure of the former president's power, view him as a direct report.

Months later, the vice president resigns, citing "family reasons." The former president is appointed as vice president of the United States and confirmed by Congress. Then, a crisis—such as a terror attack, market crash, or cyber blackout—strikes. The sitting president, claiming ill health, steps down. Under the *Presidential Succession Act of 1947*, the vice president becomes president. The situation is akin to that of President Gerald Ford, who was appointed vice president shortly after Spiro Agnew resigned. Subsequently, President Richard Nixon resigned, and Ford ascended to the presidency.

Litigation follows. Lower courts write confusing opinions. Scholars fill the airwaves debating whether the move violates the spirit but not the text of the Twenty-Second Amendment. "*Succession is not election*," argues one opinion piece in a prominent magazine. A newly expanded Supreme Court takes the case and, in a 17-2 decision, upholds the arrangement as constitutional. The majority opinion holds:

> *The people remain free to vote as they choose. The elected individuals resigned, and the two political branches of government followed the Succession law. This decision in no way interferes with the constitutional prohibition on being elected to a third term.*

No tanks rolled down Pennsylvania Avenue. The events were a quiet, bureaucratic maneuver that allowed one person to serve three terms as president and was accomplished within the constitutional framework.

9. Two years to cement one-party rule.

With unified control of government, the Opportunity Party has two years to entrench dominance. Success means decades of rule; failure invites unrest—political, legal, or violent.

The deciding factor is Congress. If it remains submissive, America joins past empires on the ash heap of history. If its members of Congress act as fiduciaries of the institution—guardians of the Constitution rather than servants of the president, Congress can still save the Republic. If Congress can save itself, it will save the nation.

10. Resisting the constitutional coup.

Can a constitutionally structured authoritarian takeover of the nation be stopped?

Yes—but only if Congress rediscovers its duty as Guardian of the Republic. It must act as an aggressive, independent check on executive power.

If Congress fails, the burden shifts to the people. Their options must remain peaceful. It is essential since the president will view the smallest protest as an assault on him. He will not view the protesters as protecting their right to speech, press, and assembly. To the president, they are insurrectionists. The president will not hesitate to use force, even against the most minimal protests. He watches the demonstrations on television throughout the day, hoping for violence so he can "Protect the protesters."

Without giving any advance notice, Congressman Jackson goes to the floor to advise the protestors on a strategy that allows them to protest while protecting them from assault and arrest. He does it on the House floor, as he has constitutional immunity for his words under the *Speech* and *Debate clause*. He starts:

> *Citizens, Congress has failed you. It is no longer capable of performing its constitutional functions. It can no longer operate as a check on the president. It is up to you to save the nation. As I analyze the situation, you have three options that, if exercised in large numbers, will at least slow the drift toward authoritarianism. The options are:*
>
> - ***Vote out every incumbent.*** *Elect representatives who will defend Congress as the nation's primary lawmaking body. They will limit the president's power by withholding the power of the purse.*
> - ***Organize a mass protest.*** *A "No Kings" movement of 50–75 million citizens pressing Congress to restore balance. All protests must be held blocks from any federal facility so that you do not give the president the ability to use military force against you on the claim that he is protecting federal property.*
> - ***Practice peaceful civil disobedience.*** *As Gandhi taught, refusing to cooperate with injustice can halt it. If Congress can shut down the government for politics, citizens can shut it down to preserve liberty. Your collective non-participation through a nationwide work strike and boycotts of companies that support the authoritarian government will deny the system the money and labor it needs to operate. Remember also, the federal government is broke. It is funded by tax money paid by citizens through their*

employers every week. Without that money, it cannot operate unless it sells bonds that hopefully you will not buy.

Citizens, you must always be mindful that this is a fight to 'Preserve the Republic.' Nothing is the law until Congress writes it.
God save America. Congressman Jay Jackson (Opposition Party)

The coming chapters turn from warning to evidence. "The Ghost of Politics Yet to Come" is not imagination alone—it is the product of decades of viewing Congress as willing to surrender its authority. From budget control to war powers, from the Administrative State to presidential emergency decrees, Congress has steadily exchanged constitutional responsibility for political convenience. Each abdication strengthened the executive and weakened the only branch designed to represent the people directly.

Part II begins that examination. It traces how congressional habits—granting massive subsidies to buy votes, creating legal complexities, delegating powers, subservience to political necessity, and dependence on presidential action—transformed the world's greatest deliberative body into a mere spectator to presidential power. Understanding how Congress made itself irrelevant is the first step toward restoring its role as the Guardian of the Republic.

PART II

CONGRESS MAKES ITSELF IRRELEVANT

CHAPTER 3

CONGRESS CREATED A SUBSIDY SOCIETY IT CANNOT MANAGE OR AFFORD

A subsidy is government financial assistance to help a person or an industry operate or compete. In the U.S., subsidies are a form of money laundering by which Congress collects money from many and gives it to a few.

The institution of Congress has created a society that the nation can no longer afford. This should concern every citizen who values long-term stability and their children's future, as it is too vast to be managed by the president, even with 2.3 million civilian employees assisting. Over time, Congress and successive presidents have bought off nearly every business and advocacy group in the country. In doing so, the United States has accumulated a debt unlikely ever to be repaid.

More concerning, however, is what happens if the federal government defaults on that debt, if foreign nations stop purchasing U.S. bonds, or—worst of all—if rival countries create a competing global reserve currency. These are not hypothetical concerns but real threats that could jeopardize the nation's economic security and future prosperity. Congress must confront these matters before a crisis becomes a catastrophe.

Every member of Congress should ask: *How does the continued mismanagement of the federal government align with my reasons for wanting to serve in Congress?*

Congress exercises its taxing, borrowing, and spending powers to subsidize nearly all economic activity in the nation. The president uses his executive and regulatory authority to extend control over as many aspects of the economy and society as possible. Together, they extract more than $5 trillion annually from taxpayers and redistribute that wealth to individuals and corporations willing to act as the government directs.

The federal government's tax and redistribution system has become little more than a money-laundering operation for political allies. Its distribution mechanism includes tax expenditures, exclusions, exemptions, deductions, credits, preferential rates, and deferred liabilities—all designed to favor those with the power or proximity to influence policy.

While the Constitution created a federal government of limited powers, those who have held its offices have relentlessly expanded them. Whenever Washington cannot achieve its goals through its taxing and spending powers, it relies on its borrowing authority. The federal government has mastered the art of borrowing to paper over its $38 trillion national debt.

Despite being the most indebted nation on earth, Washington continues to subsidize some of the wealthiest industries and professions—medicine, higher education, technology, farming, and major non-profits. These subsidies create the illusion of prosperity in a nation that is *de facto* bankrupt, funding current benefits by shifting its costs to future generations.

Subsidies now touch nearly every aspect of modern life. Taxpayers can deduct mortgage interest and charitable contributions, including those made to tax-exempt universities. Employer-provided healthcare is excluded from taxable income. Hedge-fund managers benefit from preferential treatment of capital gains and carried interest. A Cato Institute study found more than 2,000 federal subsidies for individuals and businesses in 2010; by 2023, that number had risen to 2,418.

The Presidential campaign.

The 2024 presidential campaign illustrated a political bidding war for votes—and control of the nation's purse. Both major parties competed to promise ever-larger subsidies while claiming to defend free markets.

Vice President Harris pledged housing subsidies for first-time homebuyers, paid medical leave for all workers, tax credits for healthcare, expanded childcare credits, and continuation of most provisions of Trump's 2017 *Tax Cuts and Jobs Act.* While Harris planned to offset some of these cuts with higher taxes on the wealthy, her proposals were projected to increase federal deficits by $3.5 trillion.

Trump outbid her. He promised "no taxes" on tips, overtime pay, or Social Security income, along with a full extension of his 2017 tax cuts. To offset these giveaways, he vowed to repeal Biden's clean-energy programs and impose steep tariffs on imports. Analysts estimated his proposals would add $7.5 trillion to the national debt.

Trump won the 2024 election and immediately pressured his wholly owned Congress to pass what he called his *One Big, Beautiful Bill* (OBBB) by July 4, 2025. The OBBB, he claimed, would dramatically cut taxes for all Americans. Congress dutifully complied, passing what Trump hailed as the largest tax cut in American history, even meeting his arbitrary Independence Day deadline.

The Congressional Budget Office (CBO) estimates that the OBBB will add $3.4 trillion to the national debt over a decade, a deceptively low number. If current spending, including interest, continues, the national debt will reach $52 trillion by 2035. To fund Trump's tax breaks, which primarily benefit the wealthy, Congress cut Medicaid—the health program for low-income Americans—and food assistance by $1 trillion, eliminating coverage for an estimated 10 million people by 2034. At the same time, Congress repealed most of Biden's multibillion-dollar green-energy subsidies as a pay for.

With this overview of how Congress taxes, spends, and shifts today's costs onto tomorrow's taxpayers, it is worth examining who benefits from these government-financed transfers of wealth.

The medical profession – guaranteed prosperity.

No profession in America is more insulated from market discipline—or more dependent on government subsidies—than medicine. Federal health-care spending guarantees physicians and hospitals a steady flow of income, while the tax code shields the single largest form of compensation in the country: employer-sponsored health insurance.

The numbers make the point unmistakable. The exclusion of employer-provided health coverage from taxable income—an off-budget tax expenditure invisible to most Americans—costs the Treasury an estimated $330 billion per year, making it one of the most expensive subsidies in the entire federal code. That subsidy alone equals more than the federal government spends on all higher-education support combined.

On top of that, federal healthcare programs have become a financial colossus. In 2024, Washington spent nearly $1.7 trillion on health care:

- $759 billion for Medicaid, CHIP, and Affordable Care Act subsidies, and
- $910 billion for Medicare.

This torrent of public money ensures that providers are paid—handsomely—regardless of whether their patients could ever afford the service on their own. Meanwhile, the poorest Americans, the very people these subsidies are ostensibly designed to help, are often forced to pay full, unsubsidized prices if they fall outside bureaucratic eligibility categories.

The result is a medical profession whose prosperity is guaranteed. American physicians now earn an average of $352,000 a year, far above their peers abroad: $273,000 in Canada, $160,000 in Germany, $64,000 in Italy, $44,000 in Portugal, and $19,000 in Mexico. U.S doctors are not merely well-compensated; they are the most heavily subsidized high-income earners in the world, supported by a system that shields costs, hides subsidies, and excludes taxpayers from any meaningful control over what they are required to fund.

Universities: teaching and profiting from socialism.

Universities do not merely benefit from government support—they are built on it. Federal agencies now supply more than half of all university research funding, sending roughly $90 billion a year to campuses that insist they are independent of government influence even as they depend on its money for survival. A handful of elite institutions dominate this system: Johns Hopkins takes more than $3.4 billion, the University of Michigan almost $1.9 billion, and the University of Pennsylvania nearly $1.7 billion. These subsidies are not incidental; they are the lifeblood of prestige in higher education.

The academic world is further sustained by a vast network of federal benefits—Pell Grants, GI Bill tuition payments, student-loan subsidies, work-study programs, and the tax preferences attached to education savings, charitable donations, scholarship income, employer education benefits, and 529 plans. Depending on scoring, these supports amount to $150–$220 billion every year, a level of public financing unmatched by any other private sector in America. Meanwhile, universities avoid paying local property taxes, shifting the burden of public services onto ordinary citizens.

When this river of education subsidies is combined with federal healthcare subsidies, the picture becomes unmistakable: roughly one-third of the entire federal budget is now consumed by two sectors—higher education and healthcare—both shielded from market discipline, both deeply dependent on continual taxpayer support, and both insulated from accountability.

Universities may preach self-reliance and radical politics, but their business model is straightforward: they flourish because taxpayers are compelled to subsidize them. And the larger the federal subsidy, the louder the claims that the public must have even less say in how their money is used.

Despite decades of aid, subsidies have not reduced the cost of education or healthcare. On the contrary, they have fueled ever-rising prices as institutions exploit government subsidies. As Martin Luther King Jr. observed: *Socialism for the rich and rugged free-market capitalism for the poor.*

Corporate subsidies: welfare for the wealthy.

Corporate welfare is embedded throughout federal law. Subsidies appear in virtually every economic sector—defense, energy, science, and social services. The Treasury Department identified 164 tax expenditures in 2021 alone.

A 2012 Cato Institute study, *Corporate Welfare in the Federal Budget,* estimated corporate subsidies at $100 billion annually. Since then, successive administrations have vastly expanded them through Trump's 2017 *Tax Cuts and Jobs Act,* Biden's *Infrastructure Investment and Jobs Act (IIJA)* and *Inflation Reduction Act (IRA),* and Trump's OBBB.

Trump's 2017 law slashed the corporate tax rate from 35 to 21 percent, shifted to a territorial system that exempts foreign income, allowed full expensing of capital investments, and created a 20 percent deduction for pass-through businesses.

Biden's IIJA offered $850 billion in grants for transportation, energy, water, broadband, and environmental projects. His IRA distributed hundreds of billions—possibly trillions—in subsidies and tax credits to corporations advancing "climate-protection" goals. Goldman Sachs estimated the total cost at $1.2 trillion, with beneficiaries including electric-vehicle makers ($379 billion), energy manufacturing ($156 billion), renewable electricity ($82 billion), efficiency programs ($42 billion), hydrogen ($36 billion), biofuels ($34 billion), and carbon-capture projects ($31 billion). The Energy Department also authorized $400 billion in loans for climate initiatives.

Trump's OBBB partially repealed a few of Biden's green-energy subsidies—eliminating tax credits for electric vehicles, charging stations, home energy improvements, solar and wind production, hydrogen fuel, and the $27 billion greenhouse-reduction fund.

These programs benefited many of the world's wealthiest corporations. Roughly 300,000 buyers of electric cars claimed $2 billion in tax credits. Constellation Energy plans to reopen the infamous Three Mile Island nuclear plant to supply Microsoft's AI-driven data centers—backed by subsidies from Biden's IRA. Microsoft's market capitalization presently exceeds $3 trillion; Constellation's, $80 billion. Meanwhile, the U.S. Treasury is $38 trillion in debt.

The CHIPS Act added $280 billion in industrial subsidies, including $40 billion for semiconductor manufacturing. Intel—worth $100 billion—received $20 billion in aid. Most of these subsidies benefit companies making chips for artificial intelligence.

Between 2010 and 2019, Washington poured more than $200 billion into biomedical research—an ocean of public money that the pharmaceutical industry relies on while pretending it created its breakthroughs alone. According to the Institute for New Economic Thinking, nearly every new drug approved in the past decade was built on federally funded science. Taxpayers take the risk; drug companies take the reward.

And the subsidies didn't stop there. During COVID-19, the federal government funneled $18–23 billion directly to pharmaceutical manufacturers through Operation Warp Speed and related programs. Independent researchers put the number even higher—up to $39 billion once advance-purchase guarantees and public underwriting of clinical trials are counted. Never has an industry been more socialized in its research and more privatized in its profits.

This dependence is not unique to Big Pharma. Corporate America has grown accustomed to a permanent federal safety net—railroads, Wall Street banks, mortgage lenders, auto manufacturers, and insurers all know that Washington will rescue them when the bill comes due. The private sector's appetite for subsidies now rivals that of the states, which collectively receive over $1 trillion every year in federal transfers.

America has quietly replaced the free market with a government-backed entitlement system for corporations, industries, universities, and state governments. The beneficiaries call it "innovation," "stability," or "economic development." But behind the slogans is a simple truth: much of American commerce now survives not because of competition, but because Congress has made subsidy the national business model.

Agriculture: subsidies for the rich.

Federal farm aid claims to protect "family farmers," but the reality is starkly different. Washington's largesse for agriculture has exploded—from roughly $4 billion a year in the mid-2010s to more than $20 billion annually—yet the lion's share flows not to struggling small producers, but to wealthy agribusiness interests.

Government records show a persistent pattern of concentration: in 2016, the richest 1 percent of farms received 17 percent of all payments, and the top 10 percent took 60 percent. By 2019 those shares had climbed—nearly one-quarter of subsidy dollars went to the top 1 percent, and two-thirds to the top 10 percent. Meanwhile, the family farms that politicians claim to support on the stump receive a dwindling share of the public purse.

Today, federal support still amounts to a double-digit share of net farm income—over 13 percent in 2023—but most of that support is harvested by the largest operations equipped to maximize subsidy receipts, not by the small farms their champions claim to defend.

The result is a subsidy regime in which public money panders to scale and wealth: giant commodity producers, powerful agribusinesses, and heavily capitalized operations collect the bulk of federal checks, while the romantic ideal of the independent, modest family farm recedes further from reality. In practice, "farm aid" has become farm enrichment—chiefly for the affluent few.

Nonprofits: the business of doing good.

The nonprofit sector is widely imagined as a realm of charity and altruism. In reality, it is one of the largest and most lucrative industries in America—5 to 6 percent of the entire U.S. economy, controlling $5.2 trillion in assets across roughly 1.8 million organizations. Collectively, nonprofits generate about $2.6 trillion a year, and post more than $238 billion in net income. This is not a cottage industry of do-gooders; it is a vast, tax-exempt economic empire.

Behind the moral halo sit some of the nation's wealthiest institutions: billion-dollar hospital systems, health insurers, universities, credit unions, and utilities. Even the National Football League—one of the richest brands on earth—enjoyed nonprofit status until 2014. Many government contractors do as well, turning "nonprofit" into a classification that masks commercial operations benefitting directly from taxpayer money.

The myth that charities depend on public generosity is just that—a myth. Only 12 percent of nonprofits rely primarily on donations. The other 88 percent function as businesses, drawing revenue from government contracts, grants, service fees, and insurance payments. Nonprofit hospitals and insurers alone take in $1.6 trillion a year and report $61 billion in profit, all while avoiding taxes that every ordinary business must pay.

In short, the nonprofit world is not merely *doing good*—it is doing extremely well, protected by a tax code that shelters vast wealth under the label of charity, even when the beneficiaries operate indistinguishably from the for-profit conglomerates they compete against.

A nation addicted to subsidies.

America has become a subsidy nation—an economy so saturated with government aid that entire sectors can no longer function without it. Corporations, universities, agribusiness, hospitals, insurers, nonprofits, and even state governments have grown so accustomed to federal support that the withdrawal of subsidies is unthinkable. But the laws of arithmetic are not negotiable. When a $38 trillion national debt finally forces a reckoning, how will these government-dependent industries survive in an open market? How will the new class of corporate and university socialists compete when Washington can no longer subsidize their success?

Members of Congress claim they act in the national interest, yet for decades they have done the opposite. They have systematically weakened the country's economic foundations by addicting society to benefits the nation cannot afford. Subsidies buy votes, attract campaign contributions, and protect incumbents. They are the quiet currency of political survival. But each one—every appropriation, every tax preference, every bailout—adds to a debt that drains the future to finance the present. And with each year of irresponsible spending, the Republic's competitive strength is slowly hollowed out.

Every person elected to Congress must confront a simple truth: if they do not act to safeguard the long-term safety, health, and economic stability of the nation, they will make themselves irrelevant to its preservation. Congress cannot claim to be the Guardian of the Republic while mortgaging its future.

The modern embrace of permanent deficits and limitless borrowing is not ancient history. It is a recent political invention, a bipartisan pact that emerged in the 1980s and has accelerated ever since. The next chapter follows this trajectory—how both Republicans and Democrats built the towering national debt that now threatens the country's autonomy, its economy, and its constitutional order.

CHAPTER 4

THE NATIONAL DEBT: AN EGREGIOUS BREACH OF FIDUCIARY DUTY

For the U.S to survive, Congress must confront its spending addiction.

Congress must confront its spending addiction and its incompetence in managing the nation's finances. In Fiscal Year 2024, the United States collected $4.9 trillion in revenue and spent $6.75 trillion — a $1.8 trillion shortfall in a single year. At the end of 2025, the federal government spent $38.5 trillion more than it had collected in taxes since Herbert Hoover was the president. The national debt now exceeds the nation's $31 trillion gross domestic product.

In human terms, the federal government has become a bloated enterprise sustained by debt and denial. If citizens were taxed today for the full cost of the programs already promised, there would be a tax revolt. Fear of that political reckoning, and the loss of office that might follow, perpetuates the cycle of borrowing and spending that now defines Washington.

Every dollar borrowed today is a dollar our children will have to repay, risking their financial security and future stability. This debt will burden future generations with higher taxes and reduced opportunities, making them involuntary servants to debts they did not incur, did not vote for, and did not benefit from. The national debt is a pressing emergency that demands a repayment plan now.

Chart 1 below tells the story of two-party gluttony. In the nearly 250 years since the nation's founding, the last seven presidents — serving only 44 years combined through the Biden administration — have borrowed $35 trillion, or 92 percent of the estimated FY 2025 national debt of $38 trillion. Each taxpayer's share now exceeds $200,000, while the average personal income is $66,662. The CBO projects that the debt will reach 181 percent of GDP by 2053, with an additional $10.5 trillion in interest payments over the next decade.

Debt growth by administration: a bipartisan record of spending.

Since Ronald Reagan took office in 1981, the United States has added tens of trillions of dollars to the national debt under presidents of both political parties. While partisan debates often focus on individual administrations, the fiscal record shows a broader pattern: debt accumulation has accelerated regardless of party control of the White House. To make this record transparent, Chart 1 reports gross federal debt added during each presidential administration on a fiscal-year basis, separating actual historical increases from official projections. By separating realized debt from estimates—most notably the CBO's projection for a second Trump term—the table allows readers to assess responsibility clearly and fairly. The result is unmistakable:

since Reagan, Republican and Democratic presidents have contributed almost equally to the growth of the national debt, underscoring that the problem is structural, not partisan.

Chart 1: illustrates the change in the National Debt by Presidential Administration (FY Basis).
All figures in ***trillions of dollars****, unless otherwise noted.*

President	**Fiscal Years**	**Party**	**Debt Added During Term**	**Notes**
Ronald Reagan	1982–1989	R	**+1.86**	
George H. W. Bush	1990–1993	R	**+1.55**	
Bill Clinton	1994–2001	D	**+1.40**	
George W. Bush	2002–2009	R	**+5.85**	
Barack Obama	2010–2017	D	**+8.60**	
Donald Trump (45)	2018–2021	R	**+8.20**	**Actual FY data**
Joe Biden	2022–2025	D	**+7.20**	**Estimated / near-final**
Donald Trump (47)	2026–2029	R	**+4.30**	**CBO estimate (projected)**

Party total since Reagan.

Actual debt added (Historical Only):

- Republican Presidents: $17.46 trillion
- Democratic Presidents: $17.20 trillion

Including CBO projection (Trump Second Term):

- Republican Presidents (incl. projection): $21.76 trillion
- Democratic Presidents: $17.20 trillion

Based on CBO estimates, when Trump leaves office in January 2029 the national debt will be $39 - $40 trillion and he will have added $12.5 trillion to the debt, or 31% of the entire national debt will have been added during Trump's watch.

Chart 2: The cumulative national debt and why it matters.

Annual deficits often dominate political debate, but they obscure the true scale of the problem. What ultimately constrains a nation is not a single year's borrowing, but the total accumulation of debt over time. Chart 2 below shifts the focus from individual administrations to the cumulative national debt, measured at the end of each presidency. Before the Reagan administration, the chart reveals a national debt under $1 trillion. From Reagan forward the chart shows a sharp and sustained acceleration of the debt. By labeling each point with the responsible administration and extending the line to include official CBO projections, the chart makes clear that today's debt crisis is not the product of one party or one president, but the consequence of decades of compounding decisions.

The growth of the national debt has become exponential in character. Chart 2 provides the essential context for understanding why today's fiscal challenge is fundamentally different from those faced by earlier generations.

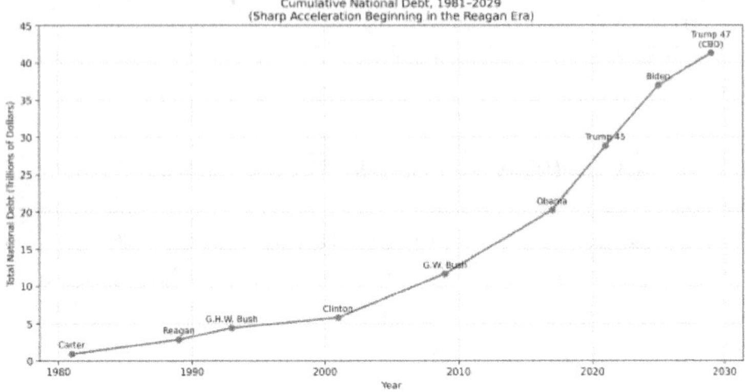

Note: Debt levels shown at the end of each administration. Trump 47 reflects a Congressional Budget Office projection of approximately $4.3 trillion in additional federal debt during a second Trump term (estimate, not realized).

Chart 3: The impact of debt on interest payments.

The primary point of Chart 3 is that prior to the Reagan administration the U.S. had a long period of relative stability in borrowing. Since Reagan, however, cumulative debt has become a danger to the country due to the high costs to carry it. As borrowing accelerates, so too do interest payments. At current levels, interest on the debt is no longer a secondary budget item; it is becoming one of the federal government's largest and fastest-growing expenditures. Chart 3 examines interest costs on the national debt, revealing how past borrowing decisions now constrain future policy choices and threaten Congress's ability to govern at all.

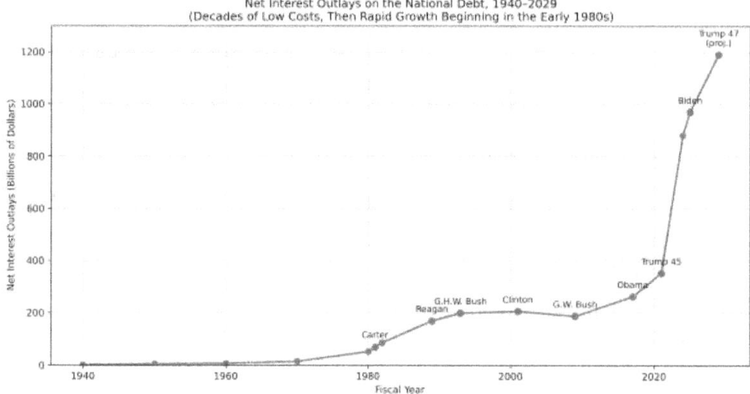

Note: Historical interest outlays (through FY2025) are from OMB data as published in FRED (series FYOINT). FY2026–FY2029 are projections from OMB Historical Tables (Table 8.1). Separately, CBO projects roughly $4.3 trillion in additional federal debt during a second Trump term (estimate, not realized).

[* **Source note:** Chart 1 showing increases in the national debt by presidential administration is an update to a chart presented in *Devolution of Power*, pages 44-45. The primary change is that the update reflects CBO's estimates of additional debt during the second Trump administration. Chart 2 (graph of cumulative debt) and Chart 3 (impact of debt on interest payments) were retrieved by ChatGPT, upon my request, from government sources and are appropriately cited. The key point of Chart 3 is that it extends back to 1940 to establish that for decades before the Reagan administration, debt and its repayment was stable. This chart is essential since the public charts generally found in the literature go back only to 1980.

****See also, Net Interest Outlays on the National Debt, 1940–2029.** Historical interest outlays through FY2025 are from the Office of Management and Budget (OMB), *Historical Tables*, as published by the Federal Reserve Bank of St. Louis (FRED), series **FYOINT**. Projections for FY2026–FY2029 are from OMB *Historical Tables*, Table 8.1. Congressional Budget Office estimates are used solely to contextualize projected debt growth and are identified as estimates.]

The big picture.

Taken together, the debt and interest charts reveal the true nature of the problem confronting the Republic. Over successive administrations, both parties in Congress have allowed the national debt to compound to levels unseen in American history, and interest costs—once manageable—are now accelerating rapidly. What began as episodic borrowing has become a structural dependency, one that diverts hundreds of billions of dollars each year before

Congress funds defense, infrastructure, or basic governance. This trajectory is not the result of any single president or political ideology. It is the consequence of a Congress that has abandoned its fiduciary duty to control spending, borrowing, and long-term obligations. Left unchecked, rising debt and interest costs will increasingly dictate national policy, leaving future lawmakers with fewer choices and the nation at near collapse.

The price of abdicating constitutional power.

When Congress forfeits discipline over money, it forfeits discipline over power. Drawing on this iron law of politics, the executive has learned that, by executive order, emergency declaration, regulation, or the proclamation of a national security concern, it can circumvent any limitation that once required legislative consent. It is now time for every member of Congress to learn that unless they protect the institution of Congress by checking the accumulating powers taken from them by presidents, they will be irrelevant.

The following chapters trace how this quiet transfer of power from Congress to the executive occurred and what can be done to reverse it.

CHAPTER 5

CONGRESS FIDDLES WHILE PRESIDENTS BURN THE CONSTITUTION

For decades, members of Congress in both parties have shifted the loyalty they owe to the Constitution and the institution of Congress to their party—and the president whenever he is of the same party.

This allegiance to the presidency by members of the president's political party has become another iron rule of Congress. Party leaders enforce allegiance through threats of primaries, loss of campaign funds, and denial of committee posts. These are pressures that few members can resist. Under such pressures, Congress has morphed from a coequal branch into a subsidiary of the presidency by allowing presidents to burn the Constitution while it fiddles.

The pattern continues under the second Trump administration. Like his predecessors, Trump accumulates power—but with unprecedented speed and intensity.

Surrounded by loyalists who treat him as a movement, not merely as the president, he "reminds" congressional supporters to *stay in line.* He challenges the judiciary, knowing it lacks enforcement authority. He ridicules or punishes anyone who speaks or writes what he disapproves of.

Trump's second term: the Drama King's first days.

Within days of taking office, the president created a high-level commission to eliminate "waste, fraud, and abuse" (WFA). The gesture masked a reallocation of spending toward his priorities and new tax breaks for the wealthy, as outlined in his OBBB. The working class, unfortunately, paid the price through reduced medical insurance subsidies and food assistance, a stark reminder of the harm new legislation can have on ordinary citizens.

To execute the WFA plan, Trump appointed Elon Musk as Head of the newly minted DOGE. Styled as reformers, DOGE operatives purged thousands of civil servants, inspector generals, and ethics officers, and drastically reduced budgets for disfavored agencies such as USAID and Education. DOGE promised to find $2 trillion in savings but could document less than $115 billion. Its actual purpose was not fiscal—it was political: the centralization of power in the presidency.

DOGE's zeal spawned a litigation storm. *Just Security* documented roughly 547 lawsuits against the administration in its first ten months. Depending on how cases are counted, the government lost between 60% and 93% of them in lower courts, suggesting widespread judicial rejection of its actions as arbitrary or contrary to law.

When Musk departed, he denounced the OBBB as a "spending explosion," and threatened to create a new political party, the "America Party." He lost his power bluff to the more powerful Trump.

Congress's silence.

While DOGE dismantled federal agencies Congress created by statute, the Republican Congress was silent. Trump threatened Republican dissenters with primaries, and leadership rushed the OBBB to the floor before members could read it—meeting Trump's demand to sign it on July 4, 2025.

The same party that once preached fiscal restraint voted to expand the debt by $8.2 trillion under the first Trump administration and another $4.3 trillion under the second Trump administration. By the end of his presidency in 2029, Trump's two terms could account for 31% of the nation's estimated $40 trillion in debt.

The elite bow.

Corporate and tech elites quickly learned that compliance with Trump's demands means profit. Those who contributed millions to the Trump Library or publicly pledged loyalty won contracts, deregulation of their industries, and proximity to power. The dissenters faced investigations or loss of operating licenses. Several media firms reportedly settled defamation lawsuits with Trump personally, totaling tens of millions of dollars, to avoid retaliation. Congress suffered its embarrassment in silence.

One voice, one government.

Today, the federal government speaks in a single voice—Donald Trump's. From the location of new professional football stadiums to recommending the firing of late-night comedians to the naming of new Rx plans, to massive new ballrooms next to the White House, nothing escapes presidential commentary, his wrath or middle of the night insults on social media. Defamation suits have become personal fundraising tools for his presidential library. Congress, meanwhile, is a lost cause. With rare exceptions—Representatives Massie, Greene, and a handful of others—

the institution obeys. Congressional leadership may hold a gavel, but it serves as the President's valet. Even the Freedom Caucus's periodic roars about debt end in silent surrender.

Citizens are inconvenient.

Many Americans now say, "My vote doesn't matter," or "Government doesn't care about me," which can make citizens feel powerless and disconnected from democracy. Empirical research supports their cynicism.

In *Testing Theories of American Politics* (Gilens & Page, 2014, Cambridge University Press), the authors analyzed 1,779 policy cases (1981–2002). They found that economic elites and organized interests exert "substantially more influence on policy outcomes" than ordinary citizens, whose preferences have "near-zero" impact unless they coincide with elite interests.

Given these findings, it is unsurprising that congressional approval ratings have remained near 20 percent for decades, as polarization has deepened and public trust has collapsed. The elite's advantage over the average citizen lies in the vast number of organizations they control and their almost unlimited resources.

The average citizen struggles to survive, which makes it difficult to participate in the political process. The top 1 percent hold 31 percent of national wealth, the bottom 50 percent just 2.6 percent. Politicians defend these disparities as essential to "job creation," while quietly reducing benefits for those at the lower end of the income scale.

Until Congress reclaims its independence, the citizens' voice will remain irrelevant. Restoring the voice of citizens in our government requires a legislature willing to check executive power and to speak for the Republic rather than its rulers. The following chapters trace the instruments—emergency declarations, executive orders, and economic controls, through which the presidency has turned influence into its command of Congress and the nation.

CHAPTER 6

NATIONAL EMERGENCIES: CONGRESS BUILDS THE ROAD TO DICTATORSHIP

In 1976, Congress enacted the National Emergencies Act, granting the president temporary authority to address unexpected crises. Every president since then has used it to expand executive power without congressional approval—illustrating that laws meant to limit abuse can become instruments of it.

National Emergencies – when temporary powers become permanent rule.

Every twenty-first-century U.S. president has declared national emergencies to enhance their executive power while sidelining Congress. The potential for abuse is enormous, as presidents increasingly view Congress as an obstacle to their political agenda.

Resolving national problems without congressional involvement has significant downsides:

- Limits a president's policy to the remainder of his term of office,
- Likely to trigger Supreme Court intervention to resolve the controversy,
- May leave the conflict unresolved if the Court deems it a *political question*, or
- Invites an authoritarian president to seize powers and dare Congress or the courts to take them away.

President Trump issued eight emergency declarations in the first hundred days of his second administration—more than any modern-day president. His proclamations include accelerating fossil-fuel production and mineral mining, deploying military assets to the southern border, designating cartels as terrorists, imposing duties on illegal drugs and synthetic opioids, sanctioning the International Criminal Court, and, most recently, levying reciprocal tariffs on most of the world to reduce the U.S. trade deficit.

Many of these actions address long-standing policy disputes rather than sudden, catastrophic events. Moreover, the Republican majority in Congress watched in silence as executive power expanded. Consequently, the ultimate arbiter will be the judiciary, not the political branches.

A more profound concern is that Congress has delegated such a massive amount of emergency power to the president that it is compromising its ability to serve as a check—let alone an active participant—in the nation's most critical decisions.

The National Emergencies Act.

Before 1976, emergency declarations arose from genuine crises—such as wars, banking panics, national security threats, or the Great Depression. Congress, preoccupied with other "urgent business," often failed to rescind presidential powers once those emergencies ended.

The *National Emergencies Act* was supposed to correct that oversight by repealing outdated declarations and giving Congress a role in terminating future ones.

Unfortunately, the statute is a drafting nightmare. It defines neither *emergency* nor *national emergency*, leaving those determinations to a president's political judgment. A Supreme Court ruling—*INS v. Chadha* (1983)—unintentionally limited Congress's ability to check presidential actions by invalidating what it views as a legislative veto provision, thus weakening congressional oversight over emergency declarations.

Under the 1976 Act, Congress could end an emergency by Concurrent Resolution, which required no presidential signature. *Chadha,* however, held that such a legislative veto violated the separation of powers. Henceforth, Congress could terminate an emergency only by Joint Resolution, which is subject to a presidential veto, and which requires the nearly impossible two-thirds vote override. In effect, after *Chadha*, once the president declares an emergency, only he can end it.

As a result, presidents routinely renew emergency declarations, often extending their scope beyond initial intent, and Congress must live with the consequences unless it can muster a supermajority to override a veto. The congressionally imposed time limits on declared emergencies are effectively meaningless, underscoring the need for reform to restrain executive overreach.

To invoke emergency powers, a president must merely cite one of the 150 statutes that authorize such powers—no matter how tangential the connection. The Congressional Research Service (CRS) and the Brennan Center for Justice (Brennan), which both track these declarations, even disagree on the total count. Both, however, confirm that the first emergency declared under the Act—President Carter's 1979 proclamation during the Iran hostage crisis—has been renewed by every President since.

National Emergencies declared by recent presidents.

Reagan – 4 (CRS) / 7 (Brennan)
George H. W. Bush – 4 / 5
Clinton – 15 / 15
George W. Bush – 12 / 16
Obama – 12 / 12
Trump 45 – 12 / 13
Biden – 10 (Brennan)
Trump 47 – 8 (CRS) (to April 2025)

Until recently, these declarations typically involved export controls, sanctions, or restrictions tied to foreign aggression, terrorism, or cybercrime.

Expanding the scope of "Emergency."

The use of emergency powers should be a bipartisan activity. While the law's flaws were latent for decades, recent administrations and both political parties have transformed a temporary authority into a tool for permanent expansion of executive power, undermining the constitutional balance among the branches.

President Biden significantly expanded the concept, using the COVID-19 pandemic to achieve his policy objectives. Without congressional authorization, he attempted to forgive $600 billion in student-loan debt, citing the 2003 *Higher Education Relief Opportunities for Students Act* as his authority. He also ordered that 84 million workers covered by the Occupational Safety and Health Act either vaccinate or undergo weekly testing. In addition, he imposed an eviction moratorium under emergency powers to slow the spread of COVID-19.

At one point, Biden considered declaring a climate change emergency. Had he done so, he could have used sweeping powers to regulate the entire economy—restricting oil exports, halting offshore drilling, or mandating mass production of electric vehicles.

President Trump further expanded the use of emergency

powers into routine policy matters such as fast-tracking energy production, forest logging, and ordinary trade policy. By acting under the *International Emergency Economic Powers Act* (IEEPA) to impose tariffs on Canada, Mexico, China, and much of the world, Trump bypasses the findings and procedures required by the tariff laws. This approach turns ordinary trade policy into an emergency, asserting executive control over an area that the Constitution assigns to Congress.

IEEPA, tariffs, and constitutional conflict.

The IEEPA, enacted to address genuine national-security crises, authorizes the president to regulate foreign transactions, freeze assets, and impose sanctions when threats arise, whether wholly or partly, abroad. Presidents have invoked it 56 times. Yet nowhere does it grant the power to impose tariffs, which are taxes and thus constitutionally within Congress's authority.

Trump's worldwide tariffs have ignited a constitutional conflict between thirteen states and the Executive Branch. Led by Oregon, twelve attorneys general sued, alleging that the tariffs function as an unlawful $3,800 annual tax on American families. California has filed a parallel case.

What is troubling is that Trump's use of IEEPA affects nearly all global trade. Hundreds of billions of dollars are being collected—funds the Treasury may have to refund if the Supreme Court finds the tariffs unconstitutional or unauthorized.

The dispute forces the Court to confront its *Major Questions Doctrine*, which requires explicit congressional authorization for sweeping executive actions that change long-standing policy. Since the IEEPA limits regulation to imports, exports, and financial transactions, it likely provides no basis for tariff authority.

The taxpayers will likely pay twice for the President's misjudgment.

Those who paid the illegal tariffs would first seek to recoup their payments from the agency to which the taxes were paid. It is unlikely, however, that the agency has the funds to make a repayment. At that point, those paying the tariffs would seek repayment through the *Judgment Fund.* The Judgment Fund—31 U.S.C. § 1304—is often described as the federal government's largest "slush fund." It is a permanent, indefinite, and unlimited appropriation that remains continuously available to pay court judgments entered against the United States and settlements reached by executive agencies for actual or potential litigation.

Because the appropriation is permanent and automatic, the specific amounts being paid are never debated by Congress. The Treasury pays approved claims as soon as the paperwork is completed. Notably, in 2016, the Obama administration used the Judgment Fund to transfer approximately $1.7 billion to Iran to settle a decades-old dispute over military equipment purchased before the 1979 revolution.

In the ongoing tariff dispute, taxpayers could face a double burden if the Supreme Court finds the tariffs unconstitutional or illegal. First, they will incur higher costs for the items they buy. Second, the automatic funds appropriated by Congress from the Judgment Fund will reimburse those seeking refunds for unlawfully collected tariffs. To cover these payouts, Congress will likely need to either raise taxes or increase the national debt.

The Judgment Fund exemplifies how Congress is abdicating its constitutional responsibilities related to spending by allowing appropriations to occur automatically.

The judicial trap.

By its silence, Congress ensures that courts—not legislators—decide the legality of national-emergency policies. If the Court voids the tariffs, in addition to any monetary judgment, an adverse ruling against the Trump administration will disrupt many key parts of U.S. foreign and economic policy. Conversely, if the Court labels the dispute a *political question*, Trump's policies remain in effect—yet Congress still has no role unless it is willing to defend the powers granted it by the Constitution. When courts arbitrate disputes that the political branches should resolve, they become unwitting policymakers. That is not judicial activism; it is congressional absenteeism.

Restoring constitutional balance.

Both branches owe a *fiduciary duty* to the institution they serve to manage these crises in the nation's interest, not their own political fortunes. While every president will face genuine emergencies, all must recognize that the Constitution grants Congress—not the executive—the power to legislate and appropriate funds. Moreover, the Constitution gives the federal courts the power to resolve controversies between the two political branches of government. If Congress and the president wish to avoid judicial intrusion, they must work together to govern the nation. Short of full cooperation, Congress can still reclaim its authority by refusing to fund presidential actions it deems unlawful.

A simple reform could restore balance: Congress should authorize emergency powers for a fixed period—say 90 days—after which they expire unless reauthorized. And Congress must finally define *a national emergency*. Presidents may resist such limits, but this reform would return to Congress the power it lost under the *Chadha* decision and ensure accountability for both branches.

Having built the road to dictatorship, Congress can also repair it by defending its constitutional duties, but to do so, it must act before irrelevance becomes permanence.

As Congress continues to surrender its constitutional

powers through silence and fear, presidents have found yet another way to govern without legislation—by issuing executive orders. The next chapter examines how that tool, originally designed to manage the executive branch, has evolved into a parallel law-making system that marginalizes Congress and erodes the separation of powers.

CHAPTER 7

THE PRESIDENT'S HOSTILE TAKEOVER OF CONGRESS BY EXECUTIVE ORDERS

The president's signing of an executive order is more than managing the Executive Branch; it signals to Congress and the nation that the president, not Congress, will shape the country's priorities.

The modern ritual of demonstrating power.

Within an hour of taking the oath of office, modern presidents begin remaking the nation's policies. Cameras flash as the new Chief Executive sits at the Resolute Desk and signs a stack of executive orders intended to signal authority and direction. Each signature proclaims that a new era has begun, and that the president—rather than Congress—will determine the nation's priorities.

Historically, executive orders are directives issued by the president to officers within the Executive Branch, instructing them to take or cease specific actions related to policy or management. In practice, presidents often present these directives as if they bind not only federal officials but the nation itself, and in some cases even the world, through tariffs, trade, or sanctions.

A historical surge.

Other than during wartime, presidents from Eisenhower through Obama issued between 11 and 23 executive orders in their first 100 days, shaping public and institutional expectations of presidential authority in the early parts of their term.

That pattern changed dramatically in the last decade:

- **Trump 45 (2017)** issued 33 executive orders in his first 100 days, permanently altering expectations of presidential authority.
- **Biden (2021)** surpassed that record with 42 in his first 100 days.
- **Trump 47 (2025)** shattered them both by signing 142 executive orders within 100 days—the most by any president in American history in the first 100 days.

This escalation marks a significant institutional shift, with presidents increasingly issuing executive orders rather than working with Congress to enact statutes. This shift underscores the president's growing powers.

Substantive policy reversals.

Each administration now treats the executive orders of its predecessor as temporary decrees to be revoked on the day it takes office.

- **During President Trump**'s first term, he revoked 20 of President Obama's orders, reversed Deferred Action for Childhood Arrivals, initiated repeal procedures for the Affordable Care Act, promoted offshore drilling, expedited energy permitting, withdrew from the Paris Climate Accord, and reduced regulatory oversight.

- **Biden** revoked 42 of Trump's orders, halting border-wall funding, rescinding the travel ban, rejoining the Paris Climate Accord, initiating government-wide DEI programs, and imposing mask mandates on federal property.
- **Trump 47** then rescinded seventy-eight of Biden's executive orders, terminating DEI and gender directives, greatly expanding fossil-fuel exploration and production, re-weaponizing immigration enforcement, and creating DOGE to do much of the dirty work of dismantling government. His orders went beyond the federal government, directly targeting private entities such as universities and law firms, and directing the Department of Justice (DOJ) to bring civil cases against perceived opponents.

Whenever the opposition party wins the White House, the nation's policies flip upside-down. The same laws are invoked to justify opposite results. The essential question arises: *how can the same statute be used to produce contradictory policies without congressional involvement?*

The constitutional limits.

President Obama once said, *"I've got a pen, and I've got a phone."* It was an honest statement that sparked a tradition of presidents boldly bypassing Congress by issuing executive orders.

The scope of the executive order's legal status is clearly set out in *Youngstown Sheet & Tube Co. v. Sawyer* (1952), where Justice Black stated that the president's duty to faithfully execute laws refutes the idea that he is to be a lawmaker. While underscoring the overall constitutional boundaries of an executive order, Justice Jackson's concurring opinion set out an enduring three-part test that defines the extent of executive power in the several contexts in which executive orders are issued:

1. **Zone 1 – Maximum Power:** When the president acts pursuant to express or implied authorization of Congress or the Constitution.
2. **Zone 2 – Twilight:** When Congress has not spoken clearly, authority is uncertain and shared.
3. **Zone 3 – Lowest Ebb:** When the president acts against the express will of Congress.

In effect, the president's discretion expands in the twilight due to legislative ambiguity. The key point is that congressional ambiguity increases presidential power by providing a window for a president to claim it.

Judicial battles and the "Zone of Twilight."

The explosion of executive orders in Trump's second administration has overwhelmed the federal courts. *Just Security*, an online tracker of administrative litigation, lists 547 lawsuits challenging his orders as of December 2025—spanning immigration and trade, the dissolution of the Department of Education, and sanctions against private law firms. Each suit asks the same fundamental question: *where does executive implementation end, and when is legislation needed?*

Since the Nixon presidency, courts have consistently ruled that presidents have broad discretion in implementing congressionally established programs, but they cannot nullify congressional appropriations or duly enacted laws. *Just Security* categorizes how the courts are ruling on cases involving Trump. It puts them all into executive actions that are blocked, temporarily blocked, blocked pending appeal, and cases in which the administration has prevailed. The cases explore the limits of presidential power.

Established legal principles.

From *Youngstown* through the impoundment cases of the 1970s, several enduring principles define the limits of presidential power. Understanding these principles is crucial to challenging the boundaries of executive power.

1. **Execution, not legislation:** A president may issue executive orders only to execute existing law, not to create new law.
2. **No suspension of law:** A president's refusal to enforce or suspend valid statutes violates the "Take Care" clause.
3. **The boundaries of discretion:** The president may administer laws flexibly but must fulfill the intended objectives established by Congress.
4. **Ambiguity favors the executive—temporarily:** If a statute is vague, the president's interpretation stands until Congress amends it, defunds it, or the courts overturn it.

These guideposts affirm that executive power is conditional, not absolute in making policy; however, Congress must act to preserve its own authority.

Congress fails to defend itself.

Presidents issue overreaching executive orders precisely because Congress allows them to. When statutes are ambiguous, the president's interpretation initially prevails by default. Members of Congress aligned with the president's party typically defend overreach, ignoring their higher oath to the Constitution and to their own institution.

Congress is not powerless. It can:

- Enact clarifying legislation.
- Conduct aggressive oversight, issue subpoenas, and exercise its contempt power.
- Demand documents from the Executive Branch.
- Sue if it can establish institutional standing.
- And most decisively, use the power of the purse to withhold funding until cooperation is restored.

Yet Congress rarely acts. Fear of political reprisal and dependence on presidential popularity render it submissive.

This silence is the very definition of irrelevance.

The path not taken.

Ironically, when the president's party holds a majority in Congress, the legislative route would be faster and safer: requesting new legislation, seeking reorganization authority, or proposing the rescission of appropriated funds. These methods achieve the same goals without litigation or constitutional strain. However, presidents prefer executive orders because they immediately display dominance and diminish Congress by projecting strength, even at the expense of legality.

A government by presidential signature cannot endure.

Executive orders have become the operating code of modern presidential governance—a system run by decree rather than debate. Presidents use executive orders to add new lines to the law; each successor overwrites them. Congress watches, paralyzed, while its constitutional role dissolves into ceremony.

If Congress ever intends to reclaim its relevance, it must reassert its legislative supremacy, defend its institutional integrity, and remind future presidents that the republic endures only when laws are made by the representatives of the people, not by the pen of one person.

Utilizing the many newfound powers of the presidency, Presidents Obama, Biden, and Trump are doing more than changing the Executive Branch; they are reshaping the Constitution's structure while Congress watches. The next chapter addresses the crucial question: *What is the next stage of presidential manipulation of the federal government?*

CHAPTER 8

FROM REGULATORY SCLEROSIS TO STATE CAPITALISM

Trump's campaign rhetoric promised a leaner, more efficient government that would unleash private enterprise. In practice, however, he is steering the nation toward State Capitalism—an arrangement in which the state becomes a dominant market participant, directing private industry to serve political ends. In this model, direction flows from one person, and it can change from day to day.

How did this happen?

Power is not dispersed in the Trump administration; it is concentrated in the President's hands. The system increasingly resembles China's, where the state exercises profound influence over corporate decisions, market outcomes, and even cultural norms.

On the first day of his second term, Trump launched a sweeping transformation of the federal government. The shift was breathtaking not only for its speed but for its method: instead of pursuing new legislation, notice-and-comment rulemaking, or congressionally approved reorganization plans, he began governing through direct presidential command.

The United States is moving with startling velocity from the regulatory paralysis of the Obama and Biden years into a system defined by one-person decision-making—powered by emergency declarations, executive orders, and the credible threat of retaliation. Trump is no longer using the federal regulatory process to make policy; he is turning the federal government itself into a kind of national corporate headquarters. Decisions once left to regulatory agencies and private corporate boards—mergers, pricing strategies, factory operations, and even federal ownership stakes—are now being shaped from the Oval Office, most visibly in the semiconductor and pharmaceutical sectors. And all this has unfolded without a national emergency to justify it and without a murmur of resistance from Congress.

The tragedy of America's transformation from the Administrative State to a form of State Capitalism is the accelerating erosion of constitutional balance. As presidents bypass Congress through emergency powers, executive directives, and direct economic control, the constitutional basis for such authority grows ever more tenuous.

By cutting Congress out of decisions that fundamentally restructure the federal government and redirect the economy, a president is defying the Constitution's explicit assignment of legislative, taxing, and fiscal powers to Congress. More troubling still is Congress's readiness to surrender its own relevance rather than defend the separation of powers. If unilateral governance continues, the Trump administration's agenda—from bureaucratic overhaul to tariff-driven industrial policy—will rest on unstable ground, lacking both permanence and the legitimacy of law.

The warning could not be clearer: only a deliberate

return to constitutional norms can halt this slide into one-person rule.

A staggering list of commands.

In less than a year, Trump signed 210 directives, many of which extended into private enterprise, raising concerns about unchecked executive power over industry and the rule of law. The President even weighs in on corporate matters as small as corporate logos, beverage sugar content, and individual plant closures.

As part of his pharmaceutical dealmaking, Trump branded an arrangement with Pfizer as "TrumpRx." In exchange for a three-year reprieve from 100% tariffs on imported pharmaceuticals, the company agreed to sell directly to consumers online at the lowest price paid in the developed world. Such moves reverberate across the private sector and raise fundamental questions about the future of free enterprise under an executive-centric regime.

Trump also issued executive orders targeting five prominent law firms that represented clients who took positions adverse to those taken during his first administration, alleging that they posed a threat to national security and engaged in discriminatory practices. This use of executive power raises concerns about the potential for abuse and the erosion of checks and balances.

Then there is TikTok. Congress enacted a law requiring the Chinese-owned social media platform to be sold to an American company or face a nationwide ban by January 19, 2025. Rather than implement the statute, Trump unilaterally suspended its enforcement—without congressional consent—and arranged a private deal that would allow political allies and wealthy supporters to purchase the company. In effect, he nullified an act of Congress, substituting personal and political interests above the laws of Congress.

Trump embarks on State Capitalism.

To control the enterprise and culture of the nation, the Trump administration has leveraged—often under threat—executive and regulatory powers to impose financial conditions on private transactions, exemplified by marquee deals like Nippon Steel's acquisition of U.S. Steel and Nvidia's export fees, which illustrate the practical shift toward State Capitalism.

Nippon's acquisition of U.S. Steel.

Before approving Nippon Steel's acquisition of U.S. Steel, the administration demanded a 'golden share'—a special share that gives the holder veto power over certain company decisions, such as plant closures and layoffs. As part of the bargain, Japan pledged $1.5 trillion in U.S. investment, with President Trump being able to direct the allocation of the funds. The golden share device, widely used by the Chinese Communist Party, compels companies to cede specific powers to the state, thereby enabling the state to exert control over key industries.

The White House has already exercised its golden share in the Nippon–U.S. Steel venture to veto a planned shutdown of facilities in Granite City, Illinois.

Fees on Nvidia's exports to China.

As a condition for export licenses to sell advanced chips in China, the administration imposed a 25% fee on Nvidia's sales —widely viewed as an export tax, which the Supreme Court has struck down as unconstitutional on multiple occasions.

An equity stake in Intel.

The administration and Intel agreed that the federal government would take a 10% equity stake in Intel by converting $8.9 billion of the previously awarded CHIPS Act grants and loans into stock. The CHIPS and Science Act provide $280 billion in subsidies and research investments, including $40 billion for semiconductor production to boost domestic manufacturing. The White House's deal model shifts those subsidies toward direct state ownership stakes in the companies.

Future deals.

- Fannie Mae and Freddie Mac—still in federal conservatorship and valued at roughly $500 billion—are candidates for a 5–15% stock sale. Superficially, this suggests privatization. In Trump's political world, it injects cash into federal coffers while preserving decisive federal control over the mortgage market—and, with it, American homeownership. President Trump also ordered Fannie and Freddie to start buying bonds backed by mortgages. Trump claims this change would make it easier for people to purchase homes. This level of control, however, could distort the mortgage market and reduce homeownership affordability for many Americans.
- The Secretary of Commerce reported that Defense Secretary Pete Hegseth is considering an equity stake in Lockheed Martin.
- Kevin Hassett, President Trump's Director of National Economic Policy, told reporters the U.S. could take additional stakes in firms, alongside Trump's plan for a sovereign wealth fund to hold positions across industries.
- The Secretary of Transportation announced that the federal government would take control of Washington's Union Station from Amtrak. The White House also asserted control of the Kennedy Center for the Performing Arts. Trump naming himself chairman of the board and renamed the Kennedy Center "The Donald J. Trump and the John

F. Kennedy Center for the Performing Arts." This move raises significant ethical concerns, as it blurs the line between Trump's personal interests and his official duties as president.

Complex policy and constitutional questions abound in these matters. It is likely that many of these issues will be litigated. Before then, however, Congress should ask:

- How many companies can the federal government control before we are effectively a socialist economy?
- How can the government remain a neutral regulator while also being an owner of competing industries?
- Will all CHIPS Act recipients be required to grant equity stakes to the federal government?
- Can a president, without congressional authorization, negotiate export fees on all other U.S. companies selling abroad?
- May the executive fast-track permits for firms in which the U.S. holds an interest?
- Can the U.S. create markets for firms in which the government holds an ownership interest or ban competing imports?
- May Congress create special tax preferences for federally owned portfolio companies?
- What due-process rights are owed to firms subject to ad hoc presidential business decisions?

These unresolved issues raise a profound constitutional question: *Do President Trump and Congress intend for the federal courts to become the ultimate arbiters of national economic policy?*

If the courts uphold these policies, corporations should expect requests for additional fees, golden shares, and equity stakes to be attached to any transaction requiring federal approval or receiving federal funds. If, instead, the courts find no constitutional or statutory basis, they could invalidate every such agreement.

By excluding Congress, a president may avoid dealing with a dysfunctional legislature, but he risks ceding his entire economic agenda to the judiciary. Worse, if courts deem the disputes non-justiciable political questions, the White House could run economic policy without Congressional oversight, unless Congress musters a two-thirds majority to override a presidential veto, thereby limiting executive power.

If State Capitalism replaces the Administrative State, it may prove even more unstable than the bureaucratic paralysis it claims to cure. For centuries, it has been stated in many ways, *Power without statute is policy on stilts.*

If the three branches of the American government are properly functioning, no president can assume authoritarian command without complicity from the other branches. Over the years, however, Congress has abandoned all efforts to protect its constitutional powers against forceful presidents. Moreover, for decades, the Supreme Court has, by granting deference to agency interpretation of the laws, limited Congress's ability to restrain agency power. The next Chapter describes how the Administrative State outmaneuvered Congress to become the primary lawmaker.

CHAPTER 9

HOW THE COURTS AND ADMINISTRATIVE STATE MANEUVERED CONGRESS INTO IRRELEVANCE

The Executive Branch did not sideline Congress alone; it also had crucial support from the Supreme Court, whose decisions have significantly contributed to the Administrative State swallowing Congress.

Since the nation's founding, presidents have used presidential directives to manage the government and extend their authority, often at the expense of Congress. This long-standing trend, coupled with decades of judicial deference to agencies, has dramatically enhanced presidential power by expanding regulatory discretion while shrinking Congress's role in the lawmaking process. Understanding this historical context is essential to grasping the current state of affairs.

Despite the actions taken by the Executive Branch and the Judiciary to diminish Congress, there can be no rehabilitation of Congress's role until it acknowledges its fear of presidential power and its obsession with reelection, which have caused it to drift into irrelevance. In the 138 years since the start of the Administrative State, Congress has only once attempted to restrain the growing power of the executive. That occurred in 1946 with the enactment of the Administrative Procedure Act (APA), which aimed to promote transparency and public participation in the rulemaking process.

Over time, however, the details involved with the APA procedure were of little interest to many in Congress. As a result, congressional inaction allowed agencies considerable latitude to effectively shape the law through regulation and guidance. Since 1946, Congress has not made any significant updates to the APA, even as agency rulemaking authority has been used to alter the intent of laws passed by Congress.

How did Congress lose control?

Congress created and funded more and more regulatory bodies to implement the laws it enacted. As more laws and agencies were created, Congress got lost in its own maze of laws and the regulations it demanded be written. Instead of simplifying laws, it began finding new powers to create more laws. These new powers involved incentivizing states with grant money to enact state laws wanted by Congress, but which Congress did not have the constitutional authority to enact. Congress merely taxed the states more, then returned some of the money to the states that implemented their requested laws.

The American legal and regulatory system just kept expanding. A snapshot of its growth from one agency to hundreds:

- **1887**: Congress created the first independent regulator, the Interstate Commerce Commission, to police railroad rates and protect farmers.
- **1914:** The Federal Trade Commission was established to confront trusts and restraints of trade.

- **New Deal (1933 and after)**: Congress authorized a suite of "Alphabet Agencies"—including the SEC, FCC, NLRB, REA, and FDIC—many of which continue today. Congress created these agencies, but the president appoints commissioners who govern them. By statute, Congress intended that commissioners be removable only for neglect of duty or malfeasance, thereby insulating them from direct presidential control.
- In parallel, Congress established 15 executive departments, each led by a presidentially appointed cabinet officer. Within these executive departments, there are an estimated 400 to over 2,000 independent agencies, commissions, boards, commissions, bureaus, and sub-agencies, depending on how one counts agency structure.
- It is estimated that Congress has enacted nearly 31,000 laws. Agencies have issued over 225,000 regulations to implement these laws, along with millions of pages of guidance.

From 1887 to 1984, courts exercised independent judgment in reviewing disputed regulations, serving as a check on agency overreach and supporting Congress's legislative authority. In 1984, the Supreme Court, in *Chevron* v. *NRDC,* shifted the balance of power among the three branches of government by instructing federal courts to defer to agency interpretations of ambiguous statutes. The Supreme Court deemed federal agencies "the experts" on interpreting congressional statutes. This decision dramatically expanded executive authority by restricting the courts' role in interpreting the law and limited Congress's role to serving as the initial draftsman of legislation.

Agencies seized the Court's opening. From 1984 to the end of the Biden administration, presidents used rulemaking not merely to implement statutes but also to advance their policy agendas through agency interpretation. At *Chevron's* birth, the Administrative State had issued about 65,000 regulations since 1887; by 2023, the total exceeded 225,000, imposing nearly $2 trillion in annual compliance costs on the regulated community. The Administrative State swallowed the Constitution and Congress.

The Supreme Court relied on *Chevron* 70 times, and 17,000 lower-court opinions cited it as authority for their rulings. *Chevron v. NRDC* became the most-cited case in American administrative law.

The court attempts to repent for diminishing Congress.

Beginning in 2022, with a changed membership, the Supreme Court started rebalancing power in Washington. Two of its decisions provide Congress with significant opportunities to rein in the overreach of federal agencies, if it can find the interest and courage to take on the Administrative State before the Supreme Court likely diminishes Congress again by granting the president complete control of congressionally created independent agencies.

The Major Questions Doctrine.

In *West Virginia v. EPA* (2022), the court imposed the first substantive limit on agency rulemaking since the passage of the APA by establishing the Major Questions Doctrine to restrict agencies from making major policy shifts without apparent statutory authority. This decision is a key step toward restoring the balance of power between Congress and the president.

The statute at issue in *West Virginia*—Section 111 of the Clean Air Act—had long been applied on a source-by-source basis. Decades later, to address climate change, the EPA "discovered" new authority in the statute to restructure the national electricity grid by determining which generation technologies could supply the nation. The court held the agency lacked authority for such a sweeping shift. The court reasoned that when an agency suddenly and significantly changes entrenched policy, it must demonstrate that Congress granted that power.

Though only a handful of Major Questions cases have reached the Court since *West Virginia*, the doctrine looms large in *V.O.S. Selections, Inc. v. Trump*, the principal challenge to Trump's worldwide tariffs. This case will determine whether President Trump can impose such tariffs without congressional approval and whether the government must refund the hundreds of billions of dollars collected under the tariffs. Its outcome will shape the balance of power between Congress and the president and define the scope of tariff-based foreign policy, potentially shifting more power back to Congress and curtailing the president's assumed unilateral power to impose tariffs.

Overruling Chevron (2024).

In *Loper Bright Enterprises v. Raimondo* (2024), the Supreme Court overturned four decades of *Chevron* deference. This decision signals a renewed role for the judiciary in reviewing executive overreach. It also provides Congress with guidance on structuring a statute to restrain agency overreach.

Yet even with these limits, Congress will remain complicit in the growth of presidential power. Opposition lawmakers decry overreach—until their own party holds the White House. This partisan double standard erodes the rule of law since half of Congress is always supporting executive overreach. Such overreach undermines checks and balances, leaving citizens subject to the dictates of raw political power.

Only a Congress acting as trustee of the Constitution and fiduciary to the institution of Congress can arrest the slide. Proposals such as updating the APA, passing legislation to limit agency discretion, or reasserting oversight powers are essential steps. The urgency for Congress to act is apparent, or citizens will continue to live under an ever-expanding, executive-driven government.

Trump tries to take total control of the Administrative State.

Before Congress could absorb *West Virginia* and *Loper Bright*, Trump's second administration moved to reshape the Administrative State under the "Unitary Executive Theory"—the claim that all executive power resides in the president. Acting on that premise, the White House issued directives to eliminate agencies, staff, programs, and funding. The president's actions bypassed the usual constitutional process of legislation, appropriations, and APA rulemaking.

Without Congress enacting a single new law, the administration asserted authority to redirect or withhold funds that had been duly appropriated, extended White House control over independent agencies and their politically appointed leadership, and began dismantling federal agencies. It encountered little resistance from a silent Republican-led Congress. Lawmakers became intimidated spectators to the accumulation of executive power.

During his second term, Trump made clear that presidential directives—not statutes—would guide agency conduct. These unilateral moves will persist until they are struck down by the Supreme Court, and even then, compliance appears to hinge on the White House's assessment of whether the court would enforce its rulings. With Republican majorities on the Hill, and a Supreme Court that granted the president immunity for all actions taken as official duty, the president seems to believe he can ignore adverse court rulings without consequence.

If the Supreme Court is to maintain respect—or even function as a court—Congress must stand behind it if the president refuses to obey its orders. Protecting the Supreme Court will hopefully, one day, protect Congress.

This blueprint now beckons future presidents: a hesitant judiciary and a compliant congressional majority create the conditions for unchecked executive power. If this pattern continues, Congress will cease to be a coequal branch of government and become institutionally irrelevant.

Trump is using the Supreme Court as a Star Chamber, and the Court consents.

As Justice Jackson observed, the executive often acts to enhance its power, in a "zone of twilight," when Congress has not spoken clearly. After a few years of checking executive power, the Supreme Court, in 2025, returned to expanding executive power through its Shadow Docket. Instead of addressing controversies and providing the public and lower courts with reasoned opinions, the Supreme Court rules on controversial, emergency requests to stay adverse lower-court decisions without providing full briefing, argument, or signed opinions. The Court secretly picks winners, who are mostly the executive.

In its first ten months, the second Trump administration filed 29 emergency petitions to stay adverse lower court decisions. The Supreme Court granted 24 of them. For comparison, the Biden administration filed 19 such petitions in four years; Presidents Bush and Obama filed a total of eight across their sixteen years in office.

The troubling consequence of the Supreme Court ruling without opinions is that the lower courts lack guidance. Cases return to them in darkness. Without guidance from the Supreme Court, the lower courts will be reluctant to rule on controversial political issues, as they know the Supreme Court's Shadow Docket is a secretive process that asserts authority without justification. It is the exercise of power without having any responsibility for the results.

The Shadow Docket allows the Supreme Court sufficient flexibility to satisfy a President determined to rule without concern for the law. The primary harm caused by the Shadow Docket is that it disables the constitutional checks and balances that structure the principles of separation of powers. At what point does the rule of law suffer irreparable harm? At what point will most of the public believe the Supreme Court has achieved its several-century dream of being a Super-Legislature protecting federal power?

Shadow Docket stays continue to allow many of the Trump administration's most legally questionable initiatives, dismantling established statutory agencies, mass firings of civil servants, and targeting immigration raids based on race and language, to continue without legal justification or any reflection on how it is harming the rule of law, separation of powers, or stare decisis. The secret processes the Supreme Court employs through its Shadow Docket resemble those of the medieval English Star Chamber which disposed of cases against powerful figures by using secrecy to bypass the common law. This secrecy freed the courts and kings to inflict harsh punishments and torture to suppress dissent.

Is the U.S. entering a one-person government?

The last of the cases reforming the Administrative State involves presidential control over "Independent" agencies. *Trump v. Wilcox* and *Trump v. Slaughter* center on whether a president can remove a commissioner, notwithstanding a congressional statute that permits removals only for cause. President Trump asserts that as the nation's Chief Executive, the Constitution places in him all authority over the Executive Branch. And since Independent agencies, at times, function as Executive Departments, the president can remove the commissioners without cause.

An Independent agency is a government body that operates outside of executive departments and performs regulatory and quasi-judicial functions, without direct political interference. The theory behind independent agencies is that they should be able to regulate technical issues in an expert-driven manner.

The *Wilcox* case involves the chair of the five-member National Labor Relations Board (NLRB). It was enacted by Congress in the 1930s. Its members may be removed only for neglect of duty or malfeasance. Trump's firing of the chair without cause is the test case of presidential control over congressionally established independent agencies. In 2025, Trump removed Wilcox without cause, asserting that Article II grants the president at-will removal power and that the NLRB's tenure protections are unconstitutional.

On May 22, 2025, the Supreme Court, using its Shadow Docket, issued a 6–3 decision granting an emergency stay of a lower court's adverse ruling against the president. Functionally, the move denied the NLRB a quorum and halted operations until the president appointed new members. More broadly, it signaled potential acceptance of a robust Unitary Executive. If upheld on the merits, the President could exercise sweeping control over both Executive Branch and so-called Independent agencies—even to the point of dismantling a legislatively created body by preventing it from having enough members to function.

Trump v. Slaughter involves the at-will firing of the chair of the Federal Trade Commission (FTC). If the Court grants the president’s full removal authority, the era of independent commissions effectively ends. Agencies that once served as independent regulators—such as the FTC, SEC, NLRB, FCC, and others—would operate as direct extensions of the White House. Regulatory policy could swing sharply with each presidential election, transforming the Administrative State into something closer to unregulated presidential rule.

Congress, having delegated vast authority to these agencies, would find itself unable to preserve their institutional independence since the president would have full power to hire and fire personnel at will. What unites *Wilcox and Slaughter* is that the Supreme Court's decision in favor of the president will again erode Congress's power to place guardrails on the president's authority. As with the legislative veto ruling in *Chadha,* and now with *Wilcox and Slaughter*, Congress may draft statutes that constrain presidential power, and the Supreme Court can overrule the statutory framework to provide the president substantially more power than Congress provided by statute.

As presidential power expands into every corner of the Administrative State, Congress must confront a stark reality: it is difficult to restrain an aggressive executive seeking control over the entire government, or a Supreme Court seeking to be a Super-legislature dedicated to expanding Executive power.

Congress is the only institution that can restructure the Administrative State.

It is Congress's job—not the president's and not the Supreme Court's—to restructure the Administrative State. It took forty years for the Supreme Court to reverse the unconstitutional growth of agency power it enabled under *Chevron*. Throughout, Congress largely stood idle, watching the Administrative State grow.

Today, the Administrative State operates at the will of one person. Separation of powers has eroded into a system where the executive commands its congressional valets. The only path back to constitutional government is for Congress to reassert its role as a coequal, independent branch of government and use all its legislative and spending powers to check the president and the Supreme Court.

Most members of Congress act as if partisan loyalty to the president and the party is the only loyalty that matters. It is not. In fact, when members of Congress fail to defend the Constitution's separation of powers structure against an encroaching president and Court, they breach their oaths. The following chapters describe the fiduciary responsibilities of a member of Congress and the institutional benefits of honoring them.

PART III

SERVING AS A FIDUCIARY IN CONGRESS

CHAPTER 10

LEGISLATING IS ONLY A FIDUCIARY POWER

The Founders understood government not as ownership of power but as the acceptance of fiduciary duty—a solemn obligation to protect the liberty of others.

Fiduciary theory of government.

Every member of Congress swears an oath to uphold the Constitution, yet few act as if that oath imposes any legal and moral duties. The Founders understood government not as ownership of power but as the acceptance of a fiduciary duty—a solemn obligation to protect the liberty of others. John Locke's warning still echoes across the centuries: when officials betray the trust of the people, they forfeit the authority the people gave them.

This chapter discusses first principles. It defines what it means for legislators to be fiduciaries of the Republic, bound by duties of loyalty, care, impartiality, and accountability. Highlighting the oath to uphold the Constitution underscores that these obligations are not ceremonial but essential for legislative integrity. To violate them is to break faith with both the Constitution and the people.

In practice, Congress has allowed that faith to erode. It funds undeclared wars, yields its legislative power to executive orders and emergency decrees, and confuses party allegiance with constitutional duty. Political parties are private organizations that owe no duty to the nation. Political parties have turned public trust into partisan property.

If members of Congress cannot exercise their fiduciary duties to the institution of Congress, the separation of powers that guards freedom will continue to erode, ultimately collapsing into a single power located in the Chief Executive. The consequences of this erosion threaten liberty itself. Every election gives citizens the right—and the responsibility—to replace those who serve faction with those who will serve the Republic. The consequences of inaction are dire. It's time citizens make a stand.

Fiduciary government is not an abstraction. It is the difference between liberty sustained by trust and liberty surrendered to power.

The original preachers on the duties of government officials.

How can citizens trust Congress when its members spend trillions more than they collect in taxes, fund wars without declaring them, permit the weaponization of justice, mislead the public for political advantage, and sustain a tax code that operates as a money laundering system for the privileged?

Locke, Burke, and Madison each argued that government power exists only in trust, not in itself. Elected officials are not rulers; they are to serve as trustees of the people's liberty. Yet today's legislators often behave as though their titles grant an inherent right to govern—regardless of conflicts of interest, corruption, or breaches of oath.

Few in Congress have likely read Locke's warning that when rulers break their trust, they *forfeit* the power the people gave them. Locke wrote:

> *Whensoever, therefore, the legislature shall transgress this fundamental rule of society; and either by ambition, fear, folly, or corruption, endeavour [endeavor] to grasp themselves, or put into the hands of any other, an absolute power over the lives, liberties, and estates of the people; by this breach of trust they forfeit the power the people had put into their hands for quite contrary ends, and it devolves to the people, who have a right to resume their original liberty, and, by the establishment of a new legislative (such as they shall think fit) provide for their own safety and security.*

Locke's insight resonates painfully today. Members of Congress often treat their offices as personal possessions, and the Supreme Court's recent decision in *Trump v. United States* has deepened this peril. By granting absolute immunity for a president's "core constitutional acts" and presumptive immunity for other official actions, the Court has placed the Chief Executive beyond the reach of law and the legislature. A president can now enrich himself or punish opponents with near impunity, so long as he claims to act in an official capacity. Congress, fearing retaliation, drifts into silence. The Court's ruling hands future presidents a weapon to violate both the statute and the Constitution—and leaves the legislature defenseless unless it can secure a two-thirds vote of the Senate to convict a president of an impeachable offense.

What is a fiduciary?

A fiduciary, in simple terms, is someone who has a legal and ethical duty to act in the best interests of another party, the beneficiary. For Congress, this means members must always prioritize the nation's interests over personal or partisan gains, reinforcing the importance of their fiduciary duty.

Who—or what—is the beneficiary of elected federal officials?

Some scholars argue that fiduciary standards cannot apply to government because no single citizen can claim to be the beneficiary of an official's loyalty. A nation of millions, they say, is too diverse to define a singular interest. But such arguments are nothing more than attempts to sever public service from its moral duty to serve as a fiduciary.

In constitutional terms, the beneficiary of a legislator's loyalty is not the individual voter but the Constitution itself. The Constitution, as the supreme law of the land, is the ultimate beneficiary of every elected official's actions. Through loyalty to the Constitution, members of Congress serve the institution of Congress and the nation as a whole. Every member's oath is to that Constitution, not to a party or president. Each legislator fulfills that oath primarily by defending the institutional integrity of Congress and preserving the separation of powers, which citizens must actively support and demand.

Every member of Congress, therefore, holds a fiduciary duty to:

- Protect the Constitution's structure of divided powers,
- Check the excesses of the Chief Executive and Judiciary,
- Legislate within the bounds of law and reason, and
- Be good stewards of the nation's resources.

Without this fiduciary lens, which requires officials to

act in the best interests of the Constitution and the nation, no mechanism remains to restrain political ambition. Each official becomes a free agent guided by ideology or gain. The result is what now confronts the Republic—an unbound government devoted to party and self, not principle and trust.

The core duty of a member of Congress: loyalty to the Constitution's structure.

The Constitution is unambiguous in one vital respect: every official swears an oath to uphold *the whole* of it, not merely the parts that suit political goals. That oath demands loyalty to the Constitution's architecture—a government of limited powers divided among coequal branches, requiring each branch to continually check the powers of the others.

Chief Justice John Marshall reminded us in *McCulloch v. Maryland* that *it is the structure of the government itself that guards against abuse*. That structure—the separation of powers—is not ornamental; it is the safeguard of liberty. Absolute loyalty to one's own institution, whether Congress, the Presidency, or the Judiciary, is therefore the essence of constitutional fidelity. It is essential to the performance of their fiduciary responsibilities.

When members of Congress remain silent as presidents usurp legislative authority, they violate their fiduciary duty. When they excuse abuses within their own party or defend the abuses of a president of their own faction, they violate their oath. Each failure of oversight, each acceptance of executive overreach, each wasteful appropriation or political payoff is a breach of trust that weakens both Congress and the Republic.

Practical application of fiduciary principles.

A proper understanding of fiduciary duty transforms congressional service from political deal-making into a fiduciary arrangement with the institution of Congress and the people of the nation. Four principles define the duty of every legislator:

- **Duty of Loyalty** – Each member must place the defense and faithful implementation of the Constitution above personal, partisan, or financial interest. A member of Congress fulfills their duty of loyalty by defending the institution of Congress itself from encroachment by the Executive Branch or Judiciary. This obligation is absolute; no member may profit politically at the expense of the structure of the Constitution.
- **Duty of Care** – Members must competently and faithfully discharge the responsibilities of their office. They are obligated to study the issues, deliberate, and act with reasoned judgment. The duty of care requires vigilance against all intrusions into congressional powers, whether spending, budgetary, legislative, or administrative.
- **Duty of Impartiality** – Legislators must represent their constituents fairly and impartially. They cannot favor one group of citizens over another due to party affiliation, donations, or personal allegiance. Justice in representation is the moral core of republican government.
- **Duty of Accountability** – Members must be transparent with the public they serve. They cannot legislate in secret, disguise their intent, conceal the costs of their actions, or hide relevant information from the public. Accountability is the public face of trust.

These principles are not abstractions. They define the moral and operational standard of constitutional governance.

The erosion of principle.

In theory, the Constitution still works. In practice, it is under constant assault by those sworn to defend it. The most dangerous attacks come not from foreign powers but from within—from officials who trade institutional duty for partisan gain.

The most visible breach of fiduciary duty occurs when Congress funds undeclared wars. Presidents routinely deploy troops without formal declarations of war, confident that Congress will fund their campaigns. The War Powers Act, meant to restrain such abuses, has become a fig leaf for avoidance: presidents rarely report to Congress, and Congress nearly always appropriates the funds to continue the wars. When the president's party controls Congress, war proceeds through executive command; legislators comply with his funding demands.

The same abdication infects domestic affairs. Presidents now legislate through executive orders, emergency declarations, and expansive regulatory interpretations of statute. When their party dominates the legislature, those acts go unchallenged. The constitutional design collapses into the exercise of raw power by one figure at the top.

When politics replaces principle, citizens are left defenseless. Rights no longer rest on law but on the mood of the ruling faction. Party loyalty supersedes loyalty to the Constitution, and the Republic edges toward ruin.

Political parties grind down fiduciary duty.

Citizens must remember that political parties are not constitutional entities. They are private associations created to control the government for the benefit of their members. Neither the Democrat nor the Republican Party has any formal duty to the Constitution or to the people; their sole objective is the acquisition and maintenance of power.

Yet, without any constitutional status, the two major parties now dominate nearly every elective office in

America. Functioning as rivals in appearance but partners in the monopoly of power, they have constructed legal barriers—such as ballot-access restrictions, campaign-finance rules, and debate exclusions—that suppress competition. The result is a political duopoly that dictates who may govern and how they govern.

When one party controls all branches, it can enact laws at will—constitutional or not. When it controls the presidency and a single chamber of Congress, it can block any oversight effort. When it controls the presidency and the Senate, it can even ignore articles of impeachment, no matter the gravity of the offense.

In those moments, the institutions designed to protect liberty—Congress, the Courts, and the Presidency itself—become instruments of partisan rule. Disloyalty to the Constitution becomes the common currency of survival.

Lower courts occasionally resist, but they operate beneath a Supreme Court increasingly attuned to political calculation. The safeguard of checks and balances falters when each branch seeks the favor of the perceived political hierarchy.

Restoring fiduciary government.

The cure is not mysterious. If members of Congress placed their first loyalty where their oath directs—to the Constitution and to the institution of Congress—the balance of powers would essentially restore itself. The same principle applies to the other branches: each must act as a fiduciary for its own sphere, guarding its boundaries not for pride, but for the people's freedom.

Most Americans, however, no longer trust Congress or the federal government. Years of self-dealing and partisan warfare have left the nation in a permanent state of internal conflict—a Republic divided against itself.

Elections test, every two years, whether voters can recognize fidelity over faction. Thus far, politicians have mastered the art of deception; voters continue to reward those who betray their trust. Yet the opportunity for renewal remains.

Within another election cycle, citizens can again replace the entire House of Representatives and a third of the Senate. Eventually, if Congress cannot reform itself, the people will face the stark choice Locke foresaw - replace the legislature or lose the Republic.

Such transformations, though daunting, are not unprecedented. Other nations have re-established constitutional order by confronting corruption head-on. The next chapter will examine two leaders who dared to put the nation ahead of their personal power. Their countries reaped enormous benefits from their courage.

CHAPTER 11

EXAMPLES OF FIDUCIARY COURAGE THAT CHANGED NATIONS

Congress is in an "either/or" situation. Either it reforms a mismanaged government and its massive subsidies to the elites, or it must accept responsibility for the nation's collapse.

Outside of wars, depressions, and national emergencies, it is difficult to find examples of government officials addressing systemic problems (massive national debt, decaying infrastructure, a poor educational system, costly healthcare, and poverty) before a crisis occurs. There are times, however, when one person—or a few—decide that the system must change to save the nation. While these leaders do not receive the acclaim of wartime leaders, their actions saved the country as much as defeating an armed enemy.

Prime Minister William Gladstone.

In the mid-1800s, the British Government, then the leading world power under the leadership of Prime Minister William Gladstone, successfully restructured a government devoted to the privileged classes into one that served the nation's people. This historical example shows that change is not only possible, but it has been achieved.

Gladstone's government was defined as a 'minarchist,' a minimalist government in today's terms. Gladstone streamlined the functions of the mismanaged British government to provide ordinary people with essential services, such as law and security. Britannia writes:

> *Gladstone was perhaps the greatest British politician of the 19th century. To him, above all others, goes the credit for creating a political system and state structure that aimed to function beyond the reach of vested interests, particularly those of the upper classes in British society.*

By eliminating the political corruption of cronyism (the appointment of friends and associates without regard to qualifications), Gladstone built an immense modern infrastructure of hospitals, schools, and water systems and established the world's first police force. He dramatically reduced taxes and government spending by allocating state revenue solely to public benefits. The Victorians referred to his government as "a night-watchman state,'' a term for a government that believes the only function of government is to protect the safety and rights of its citizens, with minimal intervention in other areas.

Roger Douglas reforms New Zealand.

Unfortunately, after Gladstone, the minimalist government theory went dormant until the 1960s. At that time, the Government of New Zealand, having funded itself through twenty-three years of deficits and budget shortfalls, realized that its prolonged debt and deficits had transformed the country from one of the world's most successful and wealthiest nations into a debt-ridden welfare state. It lost its competitiveness globally and became so highly bureaucratic that it was unable to provide many of the government's essential services.

In 1984, Roger Douglas was appointed Finance Minister. He adopted policies that resembled those implemented by Gladstone. Douglas undertook drastic economic reforms.

He believed that *the government was the most oppressive vested interest of all* because it constantly sought power and resources for those at the top.

The structural reforms initiated by Douglas radically deregulated markets by reducing bureaucracy, introducing competition to the banking sector, lowering tariffs, promoting free trade, significantly reducing and simplifying taxes, and privatizing a substantial portion of the public sector by allowing private companies to compete with the bureaucracy for public contracts. One of his more novel reforms was to place those administering government departments on five-year contracts. Douglas gave every department head a list of goals to be achieved within that period. Failure to achieve the goals resulted in the minister being fired and facing financial penalties.

Douglas was exceptionally successful. By the 1990s, New Zealand ranked third in the world in economic freedom, and its economic growth was more than double that of other OECD countries.

After retiring, Douglas authored a paper titled "The Politics of Successful Structural Reform," which described the critical elements of his reform. A few of his key points:

- Eliminate all non-essential services and programs that are not working as promised.
- Identify how each government activity benefits the public.

- The government should refrain from owning anything since the total cost of ownership is higher than leasing.
- There must be competition for essential government services. Competition can be between the private sector and the government, or between government agencies.
- Government programs must be quantified by measuring their effectiveness and the beneficiaries.
- Create a simple tax system with few deductions and low rates. Everyone must have a stake in the system.
- Rid educational institutions of the excessive number of administrators and hire more teachers.
- Hiring quality people makes the government work better for its citizens.
- Like Gladstone, he achieved his most important reform by abolishing all privileges for the elites. His theory is that all privilege imposes costs on everyone else. By abolishing privilege, his reforms could return the government and its services to the people.

How it all relates to the U.S.

The lessons from Gladstone and Douglas are directly applicable to the state of affairs in the United States. Today's federal government resembles the poor state of affairs of the British Empire and New Zealand before they initiated drastic reforms. In the future, the U.S. federal government will struggle to pay trillions in annual interest payments on its debt, maintain a strong national defense, and provide subsidies to more than half its citizens and all fifty states. Like Great Britain and New Zealand, the United States Congress is likely to continue spending more than it raises in taxes and continue borrowing to make payments to keep the government running and avoid default. At some point, reality will strike. When it does, Congress will be forced to realize that, to remain a viable nation, it must restructure the U.S. Government.

The responsibility lies with the citizens and Congress to act now, and support structural reforms inspired by these historical examples to prevent the impending collapse and secure the nation's future.

Unfortunately, the more likely outcome is that Congress will not initiate any restructuring until confronted by a crisis. Then the government will address the most pressing issues first and avoid all others. Chaos will rule the restructuring. The wealthy and other countries will utilize their financial resources to control the restructuring. The lower-income citizens will sink into horrible poverty and hunger. The dollar will lose value daily. Help for the masses will be the decades-long promise that never arrives.

The U.S. must act swiftly to avert a looming debt crisis. The real question is, who will take the lead in deciding how to tackle this situation? Without decisive action, the nation's massive debt will eventually cause economic collapse, increased poverty, and loss of global standing. Immediately reducing the national debt is essential to prevent the U.S. from drifting into failed state history.

The tragedy of the U.S. is that the trappings of power blind members of Congress and those leading the federal government, to seeing its problems. A government that cannot see its problems is the outcome of electing leaders who believe they hold power as individuals, not as servants of the Republic. Their egos, ambition, and arrogance block them from understanding their loyalty must be to the Constitution and the branch of government in which they serve, not to a political party, the elites, or their self-interest. This understanding is essential if the federal government is to operate in the public interest, not for the benefit of the elite.

While the heavy hand of government always rests firmly on the nation, the people of this nation must never forget that with their votes, they hold the power to change the direction of their country. For centuries, the great political philosophers have told us we get the government we elect—or, as the cynics claim, we get the government we deserve.

It's time for the corporations and citizens of the United States to stop asking for more subsidies and more government control over their lives. It's time for members of Congress to stop using subsidies and tax expenditures to buy the votes of citizens or the support of the elites. More subsidies and bigger government will only restrict freedom.

It's time for citizens to elect people to Congress who will permanently reduce the size of the federal government by devolving most of its domestic functions to governments closer to the people. State and local governments are more trusted than the federal government, and their services are more affordable and delivered more efficiently. Moreover, while citizens will be the prime beneficiaries of a restructured federal government, Congress will also benefit substantially. A restructuring process that reduces the size of the federal government will allow Congress more time to oversee the essential national and international operations of the federal government.

In a 1990 Wall Street Journal, Roger Douglas noted:

> *The idea that the government can retain power by refusing to make necessary and valuable structural reforms is, in fact, nonsense. It inevitably leads to the downfall of those foolish enough to believe it.*

The chapters that follow focus on how to create an accountable government. While they discuss specific policy changes, the overall theme is that Congress and the voters can make government accountable whenever they believe it is time for a real change. Once fiduciaries control Congress, the government will begin to function for citizens, rather than for politicians.

PART IV

CREATING AN ACCOUNTABLE GOVERNMENT

CHAPTER 12

ONLY CONGRESS CAN CREATE AN ACCOUNTABLE GOVERNMENT

No matter how powerful presidents believe themselves to be, their power is transitory. No matter how sweeping a judicial opinion may be, it cannot be enforced without the assistance of the president and Congress. Only the institution of Congress can create accountable, lasting federal policies, and that can only be done if citizens elect members of Congress who commit to governing under the rule of law and to defending the separation of powers.

The constitutional foundation: Congress must reclaim its authority.

Washington's political class routinely claims that genuine reform is impossibly complex—a labyrinth of programs, legal authorities, and budgetary machinery intelligible only to experts. This narrative serves its intended purpose: to cultivate public resignation and obscure the reality that accountable government can be restored through common-sense steps.

If the nation's purpose is to continue subsidizing the wealthy so they may accumulate more wealth—and the political elite more power—then reform truly is impossible. But if the goal is a healthy constitutional government, the guiding principle is straightforward: Congress must raise only the revenue necessary to perform essential national functions that genuinely serve the public good. All non-essential programs, expenditures, subsidies, and tax preferences that confer benefits on the privileged must be eliminated.

Only by controlling the size and scope of government can it be restrained.

Achieving this requires a systematic evaluation of all existing programs, determining which functions citizens are willing to fund, and restructuring the tax-and-spend system accordingly. A simplified and transparent tax code, a clear process for reducing spending, reliable government data, and effective checks on executive overreach form the essential pillars of restoring accountability to the federal government.

The Hijacking of the Constitutional Framework.

The original system of checks and balances has been displaced by the dominance of two political parties, which are private organizations specifically created to control all levels of government. The members of these political parties control virtually every lever of governmental power, including money and positions, throughout the country. By occupying 99.9% of all elected offices nationwide, the two major political parties' goals supersede those of the nation. In fact, the two major political parties, through their members, formulate all the nation's policies and control the nation's purse.

Restoring the Founders' system of checks and balances may seem daunting, but accepting the current political arrangement guarantees continued national decline. Only a Congress whose members place their loyalty in the Constitution—not in their parties or presidents—can dismantle today's political machinery and rebuild true institutional balance. The time to act is now.

For the Constitution to operate as designed, the entire Congress—not merely the minority party—must check presidential power. That is the legislature's constitutional duty. When only the minority party objects to executive overreach, it performs a symbolic function, offering the public the illusion of oversight. And once that same minority becomes the majority with a president of its own party, it predictably reverses course and enables the very excesses it once condemned.

The unique role of Congress.

Presidents cannot build an accountable government; their orders expire with their terms, and the next president amends the prior president's mandates. While courts can rule against unlawful government action, they cannot enforce their orders. They depend on the executive. If it is the executive that violates their rulings, the courts are defenseless without Congress and its power of oversight and its purse. Only Congress has the authority to establish durable laws, control the purse, and place restraints on the executive.

The Constitution also grants the states a significant role in governing the nation. Congress, however, undermines the role of the states by offering them over a trillion dollars in conditional federal grants each year. Deceptively, the federal grant money comes from the states themselves. The federal government taxes citizens of the respective states, only to return the funds to the states after deducting federal commissions for managing the funds and imposing mandates. These programs force states to comply with the federal mandates if they want a share of their citizens' money returned.

Most concerning, however, is that these federal grants twist priorities. First, they incentivize states to undertake activities that the federal government lacks the authority to do itself. Second, they incentivize states to implement some federal programs that their citizens do not want.

The framework for accountability–radical transparency. The foundation of any accountable government is transparency, the essential ingredient that builds public trust and confidence. Yet public trust in Congress is near historic lows; roughly 80 percent of Americans express little or no confidence in the institution. Regaining legitimacy requires Congress to state its objectives plainly and conduct the people's business in the open. Transparency is not just a procedural virtue—it is a cornerstone of democratic legitimacy, the means by which citizens can regain faith that their elected representatives act in good conscience.

If congressional leaders intend to implement a president's program, they should say so. If they choose to preserve subsidies or protect the wealthy, they must justify those choices and accept public accountability for them. Transparency is the foundation of consent; deception is the enemy of legitimacy.

Congress must also articulate the principles that guide major legislation—and then adhere to them. No more vows never to raise the debt limit followed by quiet reversals. No more government shutdowns engineered through budgetary gimmicks and mutual blame. And no more presidents initiating military action without congressional debate and a formal declaration of war. Promises of transparency are meaningless unless members of Congress bind themselves to the standards they announce.

Congress should also engage the country in developing national reform plans for tax fairness, deficit reduction, and reining in federal growth. The days of thousand-page bills released hours before a vote must end. Appropriations must be completed on time, and no legislation should reach the floor unless members have had at least five days for review. These commitments must bind the entire Congress—not merely serve as aspirational guidelines that evaporate under political pressure.

Accountability also requires reviving federalism by reducing—and devolving—the federal government's domestic powers. Real reform demands far more than DOGE's superficial identification of waste or its periodic attempts to rearrange bureaucratic boxes. It requires returning many domestic responsibilities to the states, eliminating program duplication, and ensuring that public functions are carried out by the level of government closest to the citizens they serve. The goal is less power in Washington and more power in the hands of government that is closest to the people.

The federal government currently owns one-third of all U.S. land. Transferring unappropriated western lands to states willing to manage them—whether for development or conservation—would reduce federal dominance, lower management costs, and expand local opportunity.

Once substantial federal authority over domestic programs is returned to the states, Congress can narrow its attention to the nation's core constitutional functions: national defense, the currency, foreign relations, and interstate and international commerce.

But devolving responsibilities is not enough. Congress must also repeal the statutes that created unnecessary federal programs. Without statutory repeal, a future Congress could resurrect those programs simply by reinstating funding. Durable reform requires eliminating the legal authorities themselves to ensure permanent reductions in size, cost, and government debt.

Flushing out the key concepts.

The chapters that follow outline a practical path toward such a system. The process begins with a simplified federal tax structure—one all Americans can understand, one that raises only the revenue needed to operate the federal government, and one that minimizes opportunities for politicians and the privileged to manipulate. It then turns to a kitchen-table approach to debt reduction, existing mechanisms for restraining executive overreach, the need for high-quality data to achieve true transparency, and the constitutional requirement that only Congress—not the president—may declare war.

Part IV concludes with a statement of fiduciary principles to which every member of Congress must commit. The federal government will become accountable only when it is sufficiently transparent for the public to see clearly what its representatives are doing.

CHAPTER 13

ACCOUNTABILITY AND FAIRNESS BEGIN BY SIMPLIFYING TAXES

In addition to funding government operations, taxes should be fair and straightforward to foster trust and confidence in government. The current system's complexity erodes public trust, primarily benefiting the wealthy through loopholes.

How and what the government taxes are political, not economic decisions.

Politicians often discuss various approaches to taxation, such as lowering tax rates, reducing deductions, imposing tariffs on imported goods, or excluding certain types of income, such as tips and Social Security benefits, from taxable income. However, these proposals often make the tax code more unfair since they benefit select classes of taxpayers. Other taxpayers must pay more in taxes to offset the benefits to those the government chooses to help.

An honest debate should focus on how to raise the funds needed to run the government and do so in the simplest way possible. The federal government can collect sufficient taxes under either a complex or a simple system. Yet, it chooses to maintain a complex tax structure, as the complexity gives Congress greater discretion to manipulate the system.

If our politicians genuinely want reform, they should model it on the original 1913 four-page Form 1040 and its instructions, often referred to as the "1913 simple tax." The concept supporting the 1913 tax was simplicity. That should be the basis for developing a similar tax structure with only a few deductions, no more than six brackets to ensure a progressive tax structure, and low rates. Congress should set the primary function to be easy to comply with and difficult to manipulate. Of course, the 1913 simple tax would need to be updated and modeled to reflect 21st-century income, spending, and business practices, but the concept of simplicity would be the basis for a new system.

Unfortunately, almost immediately after Congress enacted the 1913 simple tax, lobbyists began pushing for special treatment and tax exemptions to shift the tax burden from the wealthy to those with lesser incomes. Since then, lobbyists and Congress have transformed a straightforward tax system into a convoluted, incomprehensible "money laundering system" that the average citizen cannot understand. At the same time, the wealthy have the resources to manipulate it.

As published by the Government Printing Office, the tax code now spans 2,652 pages, making it nearly impossible for the average citizen to understand. It is estimated that the tax code exceeds 4 million words, and the associated regulations and tax opinions add around 70,000 pages. This complexity requires most taxpayers to spend countless hours and significant money trying to comply.

According to the National Taxpayers Union Foundation, Americans spend approximately 6.5 billion hours completing the tax forms required for filing. The estimated cost of taxpayer compliance amounts to $364 billion ($133 billion is for the out of pocket costs of tax preparers, plus the lost opportunity cost of taxpayers' time, estimated at $231 billion).

The current tax code is a confusing mix of provisions that reward favored activities and penalize others, undermining transparency and fairness. Simplifying it can restore clarity and public confidence.

Examples of the types of income the federal government annually exempts from taxation:

Employer-paid health insurance - $330 billion
Capital gains taxed at lower rates - $183 billion
Exclusion of net-imputed rental income - $123 billion
The stepped-up basis on Estate taxes - $113 billion
Defined employer contribution plans - $80 billion.
Childcare credits - $70 billion
Home mortgage deductions - $60 billion

Carried interest is a share of the profits of an investment or business venture that is paid to the manager of the venture capital fund. The lower tax rates for private equity and hedge fund managers benefit them by $1.4 billion to $18 billion annually. The Senate Finance Committee estimates the cost to the Treasury to be $6.3 billion.

Over $1 trillion in tax credits for green energy by 2032; however, many of these tax credits have been repealed by Congress to pay for Trump's OBBB.

The deductions and credits listed above amount to nearly a trillion dollars annually.

The disparity between the taxation of capital and labor discriminates against working Americans.

The wealthy contend that without preferential tax treatment, investment would decline—leading to fewer jobs, lower wages, and diminished economic growth. Lower wages, they argue, reduce workers' ability to save and invest, further weakening the economy. To justify their tax breaks, affluent individuals often claim the benefits primarily help small businesses and family farms, preventing them from being forced to sell or close. Yet in practice, most of these tax advantages flow to the top 10% of income earners. The privileges enjoyed by the wealthy come at a cost borne by other taxpayers who subsidize them.

The U.S. tax system, as structured, enables the affluent to accumulate extraordinary wealth while wage earners shoulder a disproportionate burden. Workers are taxed on nearly every dollar they earn—from salaries to interest income to retirement benefits—and face a regressive payroll tax that takes a larger percentage of income from those who earn the least.

By contrast, the wealthy pay lower effective rates, as their income often comes from capital gains, carried interest, or the "stepped-up basis" loophole on inherited assets. These mechanisms allow vast fortunes to pass untaxed from one generation to the next. The result is a two-tier tax system: one that rewards wealth over work, allowing the rich to grow richer while millions of working Americans struggle to make ends meet.

To illustrate this point, let's compare two individuals: the first earns $100,000 through work, while the second inherits $100,000 in stocks purchased ten years earlier for only $10,000. The working individual pays approximately $20,000 in income tax on their earnings. In contrast, the person who receives the inheritance does not pay any taxes on the $100,000 since the asset has a stepped-up basis at the time of the inheritance. Additionally, there are no taxes on the $90,000 increase in value, which has never been taxed and will never be taxed.

The federal tax system is flawed. It imposes higher taxes on wages and interest income while levying fewer taxes on corporations, capital, inherited wealth, and government-preferred activities. The federal government taxes work and savings rather than income. As a result, the wealthy accumulate more resources, thereby gaining greater influence over the politicians who decide tax policy. For lower-income individuals, saving money is extremely difficult since all their earnings go towards basic living expenses.

To the federal government, the laborer is a commodity that pays taxes.

A recent Brookings study supports the theory that the rich accumulate wealth more quickly due to less income taxation. Tax-preferred investments and business income constituted 82% of the revenue for the top 0.01% and only 7% for the bottom 80% of households. Moreover, households in the bottom 80% of the income distribution ladder pay taxes on 94% of their adjusted gross income.

There are several ways to achieve tax reform.

There are hundreds of proposals to simplify and reform the tax code. Nearly everyone agrees that its current complexity wastes time, drains money, and invites manipulation by those who can afford to rearrange their financial affairs. Those with the means—corporations, business owners, partners, investors with significant capital gains, hedge fund managers, and individuals with substantial estates—can exploit the intricate rules to reduce or even eliminate their tax liability. Complexity itself becomes a privilege, benefiting the wealthy who can hire lawyers, accountants, and consultants to shift income and shelter assets.

While every reform proposal creates winners and losers, some ideas could make the income tax simpler, fairer, and more transparent, and also encourage work. Taxes would be imposed on all income starting at $16,000 per individual or

$32,000 per family, to encourage every American to work. Beyond that, a few clear tax brackets and a minimal number of deductions would make compliance easier and enforcement stronger.

For businesses, necessary deductions such as operating expenses and equipment depreciation should remain, but loopholes and special carve-outs should not. In a simpler system, the wealthy would find it far more difficult to manipulate the code—but they would still benefit from lower, uniformly applied rates. The goal is fairness: everyone in each income bracket should pay the same tax rate on all income, which was the operating principle of the 1913 tax code. For U.S. federal income tax purposes, the IRS broadly defines "gross income as all income from whatever source derived" unless "specifically excluded by law." Unfortunately for the average American, the privileged and their lobbyists determine what is "specifically excluded by law." When this language is eliminated from the tax code, Congress can then enact a fair tax code.

Decluttering the tax code is essential to restoring trust in government. Today's tax system stands as a constant symbol of perceived unfairness. Whether that unfairness is real or exaggerated, 56% of Americans believe the system is "complex, incomprehensible, and unfair." Sixty percent believe that corporations and wealthy individuals do not pay their fair share. These views are fueled by well-publicized stories of billionaires and large corporations paying taxes at astonishingly low rates—or nothing at all.

If Americans are to believe their government treats citizens equitably, the nation must adopt a broad, simple tax system that raises a reasonable share of revenue from nearly all citizens according to their income. Such a system would replace today's opaque code with a transparent method for financing government operations—one designed to fund the primary operations of government, not reward powerful interests or advance political agendas.

The truth is that the wealthy will always seek to minimize their tax burdens. But under a simplified system, they would pay taxes on all income, from all sources. The same principle would apply to every bracket and to everyone who files a return.

This debate is not just about dollars—it is about dignity. It concerns how a nation values the people who sustain it: teachers, nurses, service workers, and millions of others who keep communities functioning. The powerful should not reduce these citizens to second-class status simply because they lack the wealth or access to influence tax policy.

Reforming the tax code to eliminate favoritism toward the wealthy is not an attack on success—it is an affirmation of fairness. It is an act of respect for all who contribute to America's prosperity, ensuring that government serves every citizen with equal regard and justice.

The next chapter presents a kitchen-table framework for reducing spending and debt. The framework is simple and workable—but it cannot supply the courage Congress so often lacks. Only citizens can do that by studying candidates carefully and electing only those who will act as fiduciaries of Congress and faithful stewards of the Constitution.

CHAPTER 14

ACCOUNTABILITY REQUIRES SUBSTANTIALLY REDUCING THE NATIONAL DEBT

Blessed are the young, for they shall inherit the national debt.

— President Herbert Hoover

Thirty-eight trillion dollars in debt is not a warning—it is a breaking point. The United States will not repay it. If Congress refuses to act, future generations will face crushing poverty, economic turmoil, soaring taxes, vanishing government services, and, ultimately, a federal government unable to function. Yet Congress continues to drift in chaos, shredding its own rules and spending with abandon. Its only governing principle is inertia—spend first, and plan to leave office before the consequences arise.

America is steering toward fiscal collapse. Only Congress can pull the nation back, and time is almost gone. The plan outlined in this chapter anticipates the political resistance ahead. It offers, however, a commonsense approach to building bipartisan support—because without broad commitment, no reform will survive.

The federal balance sheet is a flashing red light: $5.6 trillion in assets against $38 trillion in debt and nearly $6 trillion in yearly spending. No nation can survive that math. Real recovery demands deep spending cuts, the sale or transfer of federal assets, and a revival of federalism so states—not Washington—assume more policy and fiscal responsibility. Citizens must face the truth: the federal government is functionally bankrupt. It survives only because it can seize tax withholdings before workers see their paychecks and print whatever money it needs to delay the day of reckoning. Washington is writing checks on an empty account—and the American people must force an end to that deception.

A credible rescue plan cannot be complex. It must be simple enough to explain at the kitchen table so every citizen can understand what is at stake and judge whether their representatives have the courage to act. A clear, practical "Kitchen Table Plan" is the nation's last realistic path to avoid fiscal disaster.

The Kitchen Table Plan.

Point 1 – Distinguish essential from non-essential programs.

Each authorizing committee should be required to rank its programs according to national necessity. The budget and appropriations committees would then fund these programs in priority order until available tax revenue is fully allocated. When the money is exhausted, lower-ranked programs would not receive funding. If Congress chooses to fund any non-essential program beyond that point, it should publicly identify the program, disclose its cost, and the full Congress should vote to keep or terminate the specific, non-essential program. This level of transparency strengthens accountability and helps rebuild public trust by demonstrating that taxpayer dollars are being managed responsibly—and by making clear who is responsible when they are not.

Point 2 – Sell non-essential federal assets.

Congress should inventory all federal assets—buildings, land, natural resources, and mineral rights—and designate which are essential to national operations. Selling to the highest bidder or gifting non-essential assets to state or local governments through a transparent, publicly supervised process will generate revenue directly for debt reduction, while providing tangible benefits such as reduced liabilities and maintenance costs.

Point 3 – Do not fund laws that have not been reauthorized.

The Congressional Budget Office reports that, in FY 2024, $516 billion in appropriations funded 491 laws whose authorizations had expired. House and Senate rules forbid this, yet Congress routinely "deems" such programs reauthorized without oversight into their workability. If there is no time for oversight, there should be no funding. Enforcing existing rules alone would eliminate hundreds of billions in unjustified spending.

Point 4 – Review the Judgment Fund: Congress's hidden slush fund.

This permanent, unlimited Treasury account that disburses funds to automatically pay court judgments and settlements against the United States. It has financed everything from a $1.25 billion farm-discrimination settlement to a $1.7 billion cash transfer to Iran. Until 2018, it even paid harassment settlements for members of Congress.

Secret government trust funds invite abuse. If the Supreme Court affirms lower court rulings in *S.O.V. Solutions v. Trump*, the Court will invalidate Trump's "Liberation Day" tariffs. Hundreds of billions in refunds could be paid from the Fund without Congress voting on the payments. Requiring congressional approval for each payment, as was the case before 1956, would restore transparency and financial control over the billions of dollars in taxpayer money spent by the federal government without oversight, and many times, as a payment for its illegal conduct.

Point 5 – Implement GAO's Generally Accepted Accounting Principles (GAAP).

The GAO routinely identifies trillions in waste, fraud, and improper payments. One GAO study estimates $2.8 trillion in improper payments have been made since 2003. Congress mandates these GAAP audits, but the executive rarely acts on their findings. Every member of Congress and the relevant members of the administration should read the GAO reports. Congress must regularly perform oversight of the administration to ensure full implementation of GAO's GAAP recommendations.

Moreover, a 2024 GAO report identified 16 federal agencies that reported a total estimate of about $162 billion in improper payments across 68 programs. Of these payments, approximately 84% were a direct result of overpayments. Just focusing on agency overpayments would save trillions over a decade. By demanding that the administration address the GAO finding of $162 billion in improper payments reported across 16 agencies in 2024, the federal government could save more than most new taxes could ever raise.

Point 6 – Government must operate only for public purposes.

Federal money must serve the nation, not private interests. The Founders understood public funds as a public trust: Madison warned that appropriations must be limited to *objects of national, not local or private, beneficence*, and Jefferson cautioned that dispensing federal money to favored groups would produce *perpetual debt and entanglement*. For much of the 19th century, Congress generally adhered to this principle.

That restraint faded in the 20th century when the Supreme Court adopted an expansive view of the "public purpose" doctrine. In cases such as *Helvering v. Davis* (1937), and *Carmichael v. Southern Coal & Coke Co.* (1937), the Court upheld broad spending programs and made clear that, so long as Congress enacted an appropriation, it would presume that a public purpose existed. This effectively removed any constitutional limit on federal subsidies, paving the way for today's vast system of grants, tax credits, and subsidized loans benefiting corporations, nonprofit enterprises, and advocacy groups.

Congress should restore the original understanding: public funds must serve truly public purposes—or not be spent at all. Halting the flow of federal gifts to corporate interests is essential to regaining fiscal discipline and constitutional legitimacy.

Point 7 – Reconstitute the Joint Committee on Reduction of Non-Essential Expenditures.

From 1941 to 1974, this bipartisan committee—created under the authority of the Budget and Accounting Act of 1921—systematically identified unnecessary federal spending during both wartime and peacetime. Its mandate was straightforward: examine federal programs, pinpoint waste, and propose specific reductions. Over three decades, the Joint

Committee submitted hundreds of recommendations, many of which were adopted, saving taxpayers substantial sums.

Reestablishing this committee would give Congress a disciplined, institutional mechanism for reviewing programs across the federal government. A revived Joint Committee could annually produce a single package of recommended cuts, submitted to Congress for a mandatory up-or-down vote. This process would force every member to take a clear position on fiscal responsibility and provide taxpayers with a transparent record of who genuinely supports reducing waste—and who does not.

Point 8 – Apply the BRAC model to general appropriations.

The Base Realignment and Closure Commission (BRAC), used from 1988 to 2005, succeeded because it removed politics from base-closing decisions. BRAC conducted independent analyses, released publicly vetted recommendations, and—crucially—its entire package took effect automatically unless Congress passed a formal Resolution of Disapproval. This structure prevented members from protecting parochial interests while still allowing Congress to retain ultimate constitutional authority.

Extending this model beyond defense would allow Congress to authorize an independent commission to review all federal agencies and their programs, and propose targeted reductions, consolidations, and eliminations. The full package would then be submitted to Congress for an up-or-down vote, taking effect unless Congress affirmatively blocked it. Such an approach would depoliticize the budget process, provide transparency, and make waste reduction the default outcome while preserving Congress's role as the final decision-maker.

Point 9 – Devolve most federal domestic programs to the states.

The devolution of federal power to the states will become increasingly likely in the coming decade. With an unsustainable national debt and repeated credit downgrades, the federal government can no longer borrow and spend at its current pace. As fiscal pressures intensify, Washington will be forced to scale back or terminate domestic programs in order to preserve funding for essential national functions. One of the earliest casualties will be federal grants to states—programs Congress authorizes but often lacks the constitutional authority or administrative capacity to implement directly.

In 2022, the federal government distributed roughly $1.2 trillion in subsidies to state and local governments. The process is structurally inefficient: Washington collects tax revenues from residents, filters those funds through layers of federal bureaucracy, and then returns a portion to the states—typically with complex conditions attached. States would be financially stronger and more accountable if they taxed their own citizens to support programs aligned with local priorities, rather than relying on federal dollars that come with bureaucratic strings.

When this fiscal reckoning arrives, devolving federal power and responsibility back to the states will not only be a practical necessity but an essential restoration of constitutional balance. State governments are closer to the people and can respond more effectively and transparently to local needs.

Ideally, this transition should occur *before* a crisis forces it. The federal government and the states should negotiate a clear division of responsibilities, including the costs involved and the programs to be transferred or discontinued. A detailed framework for such a negotiated process appears in Chapter 21 of *Devolution of Power: Rolling Back the Federal State to Preserve the Republic*.

The core purpose of devolution is twofold: to relieve federal fiscal mismanagement and to strengthen democratic governance by moving services to the level of government best able to administer them efficiently and responsively. States will need to decide which federal programs to continue, which to modify, and which to abandon entirely. Every unnecessary program and every excess layer of bureaucracy eliminated will reduce costs and enhance accountability.

The federal government has created more programs, mandates, and administrative complexity than it can credibly manage. Devolution of federal domestic power is essential for allowing Washington to concentrate on its highest constitutional responsibilities—national defense, foreign affairs, currency, and the regulation of interstate and international commerce—while empowering states to govern more effectively at home.

Point 10 – Control the national debt by selling select high-value assets.

A 2017 study by the Independent Institute, *Liquidating Federal Assets*, estimated that federal oil and gas reserves could be worth up to $56 trillion at 2016 prices. Even recognizing that such estimates depend heavily on market conditions, technology, extraction costs, and regulatory constraints, it is clear that the United States possesses vast mineral and energy resources beneath federal lands. Responsible development and sale of a portion of these assets—whether through long-term leases, royalties, or strategic divestiture—could generate substantial revenue and meaningfully reduce the national debt.

Selling even a modest share, far below one-third, could lower interest costs, strengthen the dollar, and create fiscal space for genuine national priorities. These natural resources belong to the American people, not to the federal bureaucracy, and converting a fraction of them into debt reduction would enhance long-term solvency while avoiding broad tax increases or deep program cuts.

This approach requires clear-eyed realism. Resource valuations fluctuate, not all deposits are economically viable, and environmental, legal, and state-sovereignty issues complicate extraction. Yet these challenges do not negate the fundamental point: the United States holds substantial, under-utilized assets that could help stabilize its fiscal position. Congress has the authority to unlock this value; what it lacks is the will. Continuing to drift from one short-term fix to the next brings fiscal crisis closer and further erodes congressional relevance.

From fiscal control to constitutional duty.

The ability to tax, spend, and borrow defines the character of government. When Congress surrenders those levers, whether through indolence, negligence, or political expediency, it ceases to be the Constitution's trustee. Reclaiming fiscal control is therefore more than an economic imperative; it is a constitutional duty. Only by controlling spending and debt can Congress begin to serve once more as a Guardian of the Republic.

In addition to reducing debt and managing the money citizens give the federal government, the government must be honest with its citizens and provide them with only good-quality information, since citizens rely on it for all aspects of life. The next chapter highlights how the federal government can regain the public's trust by being transparent, and truthful to its citizens.

CHAPTER 15

TRUTH AS THE FIRST DUTY OF GOVERNMENT

In America's constitutional design, Congress is not merely a lawmaker; it is the people's fiduciary, entrusted to uphold the truthfulness of government information, which is vital for maintaining public trust and effective governance.

Government truthfulness: the foundation of trust.

A self-governing nation depends on citizens who can make informed decisions. But informed decisions require trustworthy information—data that is transparent, replicable, and free from political manipulation. When government communications become inconsistent, selectively filtered, or ideologically driven, public trust collapses. Citizens retreat into partisan narratives, institutions lose credibility, and national challenges become harder to solve.

While examples of government misinformation on controversial policy issues abounds, nowhere is this erosion of trust more visible than in three areas where government communication is supposed to rest on objective science: climate change, vaccines and public health, and the COVID-19 pandemic response. In each case, the problem is not merely disagreement about policy outcomes but the absence of a consistent, bipartisan methodology for determining what information is reliable. Administrations change, data standards shift, and messaging oscillates based on political objectives—sometimes dramatically—with no underlying system that requires honesty, verification, or public transparency.

Climate policy swings with each presidency, leaving Americans unsure whether the nation faces imminent catastrophe or routine environmental risk. Debates over vaccines, food standards, and water quality are increasingly shaped by ideology rather than evidence, weakening public health institutions and confusing the public. And during the pandemic, inconsistent guidance and the suppression of competing analyses shattered confidence in federal agencies at the very moment Americans needed reliable information most.

These are not isolated failures. They reveal a systemic flaw: the United States lacks an enforceable, government-wide standard for scientific integrity and data quality. Congress anticipated this problem when it passed the Information Quality Act (IQA), requiring federal agencies to ensure objectivity, reproducibility, and transparency in the information they disseminate. But without clear enforcement, agencies have treated these requirements as aspirational rather than mandatory.

Restoring trust requires more than better communication; it requires a legal and institutional framework that compels honesty from the federal government. Citizens deserve information they can rely on—regardless of which party holds power. Only then can public debate rest on shared facts rather than shifting political winds.

When government information becomes political.

Good-quality information is the lifeblood of sound policy. When communications are objective and verifiable, they guide wise decisions. When they are weak, manipulated, or selectively released, they sow confusion, polarize citizens, and erode faith in government.

From the Clinton era onward, administrations of both parties have treated information less as a public responsibility and more as political weaponry. Each new president reframes data and communicates information to justify pre-chosen policies. Facts become malleable instruments for gaining votes and campaign money rather than tools for solving problems. The result is a permanent culture of controversy in which national challenges, however urgent, remain unresolved.

Case studies in the corruption of knowledge and the distortion of public policy.

1. The climate change debate clearly illustrates the need for a standard that mandates consistent, good quality information that can be tested against facts.

Since 1993, the federal government has funded thousands of climate studies and spent roughly a trillion dollars on climate change research, along with another trillion subsidizing green technologies. Yet after three decades, public understanding of climate science remains fragmented, and federal policy continues to swing sharply with each new administration.

Much of this inconsistency stems from the fact that most climate policy has been made not through legislation but through executive orders and agency regulations—actions that can be, and often are, reversed by the next president. Congress has largely retreated to partisan messaging, abandoning any attempt to create a stable, bipartisan framework for evaluating conflicting scientific claims or communicating risks to the public.

Compounding the problem, federal agencies frequently fund studies through grants to organizations that align with their preferred policy direction, while only a portion of this research undergoes rigorous independent peer review or transparent data verification. The result is a public communications environment that is often more political than scientific. One side warns of imminent catastrophe; the other assures the public that economic growth alone will resolve environmental risks. Neither approach fosters trust.

If the government expects citizens to take climate risks, or any government data on controversial issues, seriously—or to dismiss them responsibly—it must speak with honesty and methodological clarity. Only transparent data, consistent standards of scientific review, and durable bipartisan oversight can restore credibility to a debate that has become more polarized than informative.

Unfortunately, our presidents are the primary cause of the major policy flip-flops, and our Congress fails to impose standards for the communication of government information. A few examples solidify this point.

Paris Climate Agreement (2015–2025):

- **2015 (Obama):** U.S. joins the Paris Agreement through executive action, committing to major emissions reductions.
- **2017 (Trump):** U.S. withdraws, arguing Paris harms economic competitiveness.
- **2021 (Biden):** U.S. re-enters the agreement on his first day in office.
- **2025 (Trump):** U.S. withdraws from the agreement on Day One in office.

The U.S. changed its policy position on global climate change four times without a single act of Congress.

Clean Power Plan vs. Affordable Clean Energy Rule:

- **2015 (Obama):** EPA issues the Clean Power Plan (CPP)—the most sweeping federal attempt to reduce power-plant emissions.
- **2019 (Trump):** CPP was repealed and replaced with the Affordable Clean Energy (ACE) rule, sharply narrowing federal authority to regulate plant emissions.
- **2022 (Biden):** repeals ACE and proposes a new, more stringent emissions rule.
- **2025 (Trump):** announces intention to withdraw the proposed 2024 Biden-Harris power plant regulation that was to replace ACE.

There were four different federal power plant emissions strategies in ten years. Not one strategy was the product of Congress.

Social Cost of Carbon (SCC):

- **2016 (Obama):** SCC set a $42 per ton benefit for reducing carbon emissions. It was used widely by the federal government in cost-benefit analyses to demonstrate the cost savings of energy efficiency activities.
- **2017 (Trump):** SCC reduced to $1–$7 per ton, nearly eliminating its regulatory significance as a money saving rule.
- **2021 (Biden):** SCC restored to Obama-level values, with a plan to raise it further.
- **2025 (Trump):** disbanded the Interagency Working Group that implemented the SCC metric and directed all agencies to halt its use unless required by law. In his second term, Trump ordered agencies to stop factoring climate change into determining resource cost/benefit decisions.

These changes to the core metric for determining the

costs and benefits of federal climate regulations were changed only by presidential direction. Again, Congress was silent on the debate.

Vehicle Emissions & Fuel Economy Standards (CAFE/GHG):

- **2012 (Obama):** Aggressive increases in fuel economy and emissions standards.
- **2020 (Trump):** Standards weakened; states restricted from setting their own standards.
- **2021–2023 (Biden):** Stronger standards reinstated; California waiver authority restored.
- **2025 (Trump):** Revoked Biden's auto efficiency targets, and reduced noncompliance penalties to $0.

In less than thirteen years, auto manufacturers faced four contradictory regulatory schemes for the production and fuel economy of their vehicles.

The point of this comparison is to clearly illustrate that without congressional action, climate policy or any other federal policy based on science, technology, data or economics, is unstable if based solely on presidential orders. With the largest "bully-pulpit" in the world presidents can manipulate data, diminish science, and disrupt the planning necessary for reliable long-term economic, technological or scientific progress. The end result is a public unsure of what government information to believe. The result, an erosion of trust in government.

2. Vaccines, food, and water: the same data quality disputes as climate change.

The science supporting vaccine safety, food standards, and water quality contains uncertainties—as all science does—but it is far more settled than the political debates surrounding it. The second Trump administration, led at Health and Human Services by Secretary Robert F. Kennedy Jr., has begun advancing sweeping changes to long-standing medical and nutritional policies without providing transparent, peer-reviewed evidence to support the changes. Assertions linking childhood vaccines to autism, describing community water fluoridation as "industrial waste dumping," or minimizing the benefits of routine childhood immunizations have been repeatedly tested and rejected by decades of epidemiological research across multiple countries and scientific institutions.

Substituting unverified claims for validated science threatens public health and undermines the credibility of essential institutions such as the CDC, FDA, and EPA. When political leaders—of either party—disregard established evidence, they replace scientific rigor with ideology. The result is confusion among citizens, weakened public confidence, and policies that fail to protect the people they are meant to serve.

3. The Pandemic Experience.

The COVID-19 pandemic revealed the high cost of eroding information standards. Public guidance shifted frequently; dissenting views were sometimes suppressed on social-media platforms; and key data—such as the effects of school closures or early vaccine performance in different age groups—was released slowly or inconsistently. These many failures, across multiple institutions, dramatically weakened trust in public health authorities.

The absence of a transparent, reproducible methodology allowed opinion to masquerade as fact. For many Americans, the result was deep uncertainty: whom to trust, which recommendations were evidence-based, and whether political considerations shaped scientific messaging. The consequences were severe, trillions in lost economic output, millions of children experiencing education setbacks, and a long-term collapse in confidence in institutions that once carried bipartisan respect.

These failures share a common root: there is no

enforceable, government-wide standard for scientific honesty and transparency in public communication. Congress recognized this vulnerability two decades ago when it enacted the IQA, requiring federal agencies to ensure data quality and objectivity. But after passage, Congress allowed it to drift into obscurity, leaving agencies without clear enforcement mechanisms and the public without reliable assurances of scientific neutrality.

The Information Quality Act: Congress's forgotten law of honesty.

Enacted in 2000 as part of Public Law 106-554, the IQA was designed to ensure the "quality, objectivity, utility, and integrity" of information disseminated by federal agencies. The OMB issued government-wide guidelines in 2002, requiring every Agency to adopt standards and create procedures for communicating good-quality data and information, as well as correcting inaccurate information. To reinforce these standards, Congress should consider specific legislative measures such as establishing mandatory sanctions for violations of the IQA and creating an independent body to ensure agency compliance.

In practice, successive administrations (Bush, Obama, Biden and Trump) refused to implement the IQA, and courts dismissed cases for lack of standing. The actions of the executive and the Judiciary underscore how the power of the executive increases over time due to an absence of congressional involvement. If the U.S. is ever to have a federal government that is honest with its people, it will happen only when Congress enforces a law similar to IQA.

1. What the IQA requires.

Under OMB's 2002 Guidelines, government information must be:

- **Accurate:** precise, complete, and unbiased.
- **Useful:** applicable to the needs of intended users.

- **Possessing integrity:** protected from manipulation.
- **Transparent:** for "influential scientific information," agencies must disclose data and methods sufficient for qualified third parties to reproduce results.

The guidelines also established a correction process that allows anyone in the public, including advocacy groups and scientific experts to challenge inaccuracies. "Information" includes any communication of facts or data in any medium. When agencies express opinions, they must clearly label them as such.

If these standards had been enforced during the pandemic, the government would have presented only verified findings, disclosed the uncertainty levels of the information, or stated that it was an opinion. Instead, it issued mandates without supporting scientific information and treated medical views that differed from government pronouncements as "scientific misinformation." The damage—to health, education, and government credibility—was immense.

A *Lancet* study later confirmed that public trust in government is crucial to the effectiveness of public health measures. Yet the federal government's own misinformation destroyed that trust.

2. Restoring trust: why Congress must enforce the IQA.

Government misinformation is not harmless error—it is intended propaganda. When officials present opinion as fact, they betray the very citizens they are sworn to serve. Because the IQA remains law, any president could require immediate compliance. None has done so, preferring to control the narrative.

Only Congress can correct this failure. It must:

- **Mandate the implementation** of the IQA and the 2002 Guidelines across all agencies.

- **Condition appropriations** on certified compliance with the IQA.
- **Grant citizens standing** to challenge inaccurate or misleading information in federal court.
- **Label government opinions** distinctly from verified data.
- **Sanction noncompliance** through defined and legislated agency budget reductions or personal accountability for contempt of Congress.

Transparency is not a partisan weapon; it is the prerequisite for democracy. Citizens who cannot trust official information will not trust their government. Congress, as the people's fiduciary, must reassert its duty to ensure that the federal government tells the truth.

3. All government officials have a fiduciary duty to be honest to the public.

Citizens do not distrust the federal government because they are cynical; they distrust it because it has been dishonest. A government obsessed with power, resources, and control cannot lead a free people. If the Republic is to endure, the first step toward accountability is the pursuit of truth itself.

The IQA already exists. Congress does not need to reinvent reform; it needs to require the federal government to enforce the law it passed and to enact the 2002 OMB Guidelines into law so that agencies have detailed instructions for implementing them. Truth is not merely a moral virtue; it must be the Republic's operating system. When Congress ensures that the government's words are truthful, it will begin to restore trust in government, without which liberty cannot survive.

If Congress is to function as the Guardian of the Republic, it must ensure honesty is the first duty of governance.

The next chapter addresses the most sobering of government operations, declaring war. The principles of the IQA should apply to all government communications, including the facts presented to Congress for its consideration in declaring war. Unfortunately, the federal government has a history of misleading the public on these matters to advance its political agenda.

CHAPTER 16

CONGRESS SHOULD NEVER DELEGATE DECLARING WAR

The gravest decision any government can make is to send its young citizens into battle. To ask Americans to sacrifice their lives is the most solemn demand one human being can make of another. Yet for three-quarters of a century, Congress has shirked that duty, quietly financing undeclared wars launched by presidents without the consent of the people's representatives. In doing so, it has not only eroded the constitutional balance of powers but betrayed the moral trust at the heart of a democratic republic.

The constitutional crime: abdication of War Powers.

Only Congress has the constitutional authority to declare war, and reclaiming this power is essential to restore both legal integrity and public trust in national security decisions.

According to publicly compiled data, the United States has issued only five formal declarations of war in its history, yet it has engaged in well over a hundred military conflicts since achieving independence—ranging from major wars to limited interventions, covert actions, navel blockades which are an act of war under international law, preemptive air strikes such as in Iran, regime change and peacekeeping missions. The United States has been involved in some form of armed conflict during the vast majority of the past seventy-five years.

Far more troubling is that Congress rarely debates the legality, strategic necessity, human costs, or financial implications of these engagements. Instead, it continues to appropriate funds for hostilities initiated by presidents acting under broad or outdated authorizations, or sometimes under no statutory authorization at all.

Presidents now dispatch troops, drones, and missiles with little consultation and still expect — and receive — congressional appropriations afterward. The decision to go to war has shifted from being a necessity for national defense to becoming a presidential impulse.

When Congress abdicates its duty, it not only permits unconstitutional wars but also erodes public accountability, making the legislative branch complicit in unchecked executive actions.

Delegation breeds endless war and debt - the legal mechanisms.

The War Powers Act of 1973 was enacted to prevent another Vietnam-type conflict. It authorizes limited presidential action when hostilities are imminent but stops short of a declaration of war. The president must notify Congress within 48 hours of deploying troops into hostilities and must obtain congressional approval within sixty days; otherwise, U.S. forces must be withdrawn. In theory, this statute was intended to constrain executive power. In practice, however, presidents view the Act as an unconstitutional intrusion into executive authority, thereby forcing Congress to legislate an end of hostilities.

In 2001, Congress compounded the error by passing the Authorization for Use of Military Force (AUMF). Ostensibly directed against the perpetrators of the September 11 attacks, it has since been cited to justify military actions in nearly twenty countries. Presidents interpret it as an open-ended license to wage war against any entity labeled a threat.

Once Congress grants such limited authority, it traps itself. To end a conflict, Congress must pass a resolution that the president can veto, requiring a two-thirds override to prevail — an almost impossible hurdle in a polarized age. The process established by Congress now makes it far easier to start a war than to stop one.

The historical record.

The United States has existed for nearly 240 years. Still, it has fought only five wars under formal congressional declaration: the War of 1812, the Mexican-American War, the Spanish-American War, World War I, and World War II. Every other conflict has proceeded under presidential directive or implied delegated authority.

The human and fiscal toll of war is staggering. A study by Brown University estimated that just the cost of 9/11 war spending was $8 trillion.

Wars of deception.

Some wars were sold on falsehoods.

- **Vietnam (1965-1973):** The alleged attack in the Gulf of Tonkin never occurred, yet it became the pretext for a war that killed 58,000 Americans, wounded more than 150,000, and still leaves families searching for the missing. The financial cost exceeded $1 trillion in today's dollars, with billions more spent each year on veterans' care.
- **Iraq (2003-2011):** Intelligence agencies assured the nation that Saddam Hussein possessed weapons of

mass destruction. None were found. The war cost $1.8 trillion, and it claimed more than half a million lives.

Wars of drift.

Other conflicts began with a purpose but devolved into endless commitments.

- **Afghanistan and the Global War on Terror (2001-2022):** Initiated to punish the architects of 9/11, it metastasized into an eighteen-year occupation and a global counter-terror campaign costing $8 trillion and nearly a million lives. Even after withdrawal, the U.S. owes tens of billions more for veterans' care.
- **Ukraine (2022-present):** The United States has already spent well over $175 billion supporting this war, yet Congress has never declared it. However one judges the merits, the pattern remains: another conflict waged and funded without direct constitutional authorization.

An endless list.

From Korea to Libya, Lebanon to Somalia, Yemen to Syria, American forces have fought, bombed, or intervened in scores of nations under various euphemisms — "training missions," "police actions," "peacekeeping," "humanitarian corridors." Courts have declined to review these controversies, invoking the *political question doctrine*, which leaves the solution to the two political branches of government. This doctrine, *de facto*, endorses executive supremacy in an era of a polarized Congress that protects presidents of their own party. The judiciary's passivity, by refusing to review executive actions, sanctions Congress's abdication of its responsibilities under the separation of powers.

Restoring accountability.

Governments make mistakes; republics perish when they repeat them. The U.S. government appears incapable of learning from its own failures. War follows war, each financed by debt and justified by urgency, while Congress looks away. Both branches seem comfortable with a cycle of undeclared wars, endless borrowing, and a pervasive lack of the moral courage to be responsible for war making decisions.

Notwithstanding the difficulty of reclaiming their War Powers authority once a president enters a conflict, Congress can, at any time, leverage its constitutional power of the purse to restrict presidential war powers, making legislative action a practical tool to end undeclared wars and restore authority.

The remedy is straightforward and constitutional: *No appropriation without a declaration of war.*

If members of Congress are unwilling to vote to declare war, they must not fund it. Those too timid to accept responsibility for the conflicts they enable — where America's sons and daughters fight and die — should step aside for those who will. The remedy is straightforward and constitutional: No appropriation without a declaration of war. It's time for Congress to reclaim its constitutional authority and restore accountability in the decision to go to war.

The American people send nearly $6 trillion to Washington each year and shoulder $38 trillion in national debt. They deserve honesty about what the government is doing. At minimum, Americans deserve a Congress willing to perform its most solemn duty: to debate openly, vote courageously, and declare — or refuse to declare war.

Only by reclaiming that responsibility can Congress transition from an enabler of war to the Guardian of the Republic's conscience.

The need for new rules of war.

Congress has put itself into a situation without an exit. Presidents start wars, and Congress can't stop them. Most recently, according to a report from AP News, the Republican House recently rejected two resolutions that would have limited President Donald Trump's military actions against Venezuela, reflecting its inability to secure enough votes to challenge presidential war powers or restrict funding for such operations. Knowing Congress has abdicated its constitutional authority over war and peace, President Trump then invades Venezuela, captures its president, holds a press conference announcing the United States will run the country for some in indefinite period of time and repay itself with oil revenues, a clear violation of international law. Trump then provides a list of other countries that he might attack – Cuba, Columbia, Iran, and Greenland.

While a simple solution exists, repeal the War Powers Act and the AUMF and replace them with a new War Powers Act, it would require the president to accept the involvement of Congress in war-making decisions, a decision the U.S. President cannot accept.

Emergencies and imminent attacks on the U.S. require a president, as the nation's commander-in-chief, to possess sufficient power to respond, as congressional action takes more time. However, these dire situations do not require Congress to cede all war-making powers to the president. A simple approach would enable Congress to authorize the president to use force for 60 days. After 60 days, Congress would need to reauthorize the president's war powers, or they would automatically cease. While this approach would require a unified Congress to enact an amended War Powers statute, it would be a statement by Congress to the American people that it is committed to assuming its constitutional responsibilities.

The next chapter on Accountability identifies the

powers held by Congress to control executive overreach. If utilized, these powers allow Congress to use anti-takeover defenses that would prevent presidents from intruding on their legislative power.

CHAPTER 17

CONGRESS MUST DEPLOY ITS ANTI-TAKEOVER DEFENSES AGAINST EXECUTIVE OVERREACH

Congress must respect itself as the branch constitutionally empowered to set national policy. When it fails to check presidential overreach, it accepts a master–servant relationship in which the President becomes the master. That surrender is not compelled by law; it is chosen.

The power struggle.

The struggle for power between Congress and the president is a permanent feature of American government. It persists regardless of how much authority Congress delegates to the Chief Executive. The conflict arises over statutory interpretation, spending priorities, troop deployments, emergency declarations, and the reprogramming of appropriated funds. Presidents routinely seek to expand their discretion, often portraying Congress as slow, divided, or irrelevant. Left unchecked, that narrative becomes self-fulfilling.

Members of Congress therefore face an existential choice. They can act as fiduciaries of the Constitution and guardians of Congress's Article I powers, or they can subordinate those duties to loyalty to a president and the political party that sustains their careers. Citizens, as the ultimate principals in this constitutional system, can influence that choice through elections. When voters reward obedience to president and party over independence, they accelerate the erosion of the separation of powers.

As discussed in Chapters 5 and 6, modern presidential power grabs rarely announce themselves as such. They are executed through executive orders, expansive regulations, emergency declarations, and implicit threats of political retaliation. Presidents invariably claim urgency or necessity, yet these "emergencies" often persist long after any genuine crisis has passed. President Biden's attempt to forgive student loan debt under the pretext of the COVID-19 emergency continued well beyond the pandemic's end until the Supreme Court intervened. President Trump, by contrast, declared nearly every major initiative—from energy policy to tariffs—an "emergency," treating unilateral presidential action as a substitute for legislation.

Congress has the power—but lacks the will.

The Constitution arms Congress with formidable defenses against executive encroachment. These are not symbolic powers; they are operational tools designed to prevent the president from absorbing legislative authority. Yet too many members lack the courage—or the institutional loyalty—to use them. Members of the president's party frequently defend "their" president even when his actions are plainly unconstitutional. When the president's party controls one or both chambers, congressional acquiescence to presidential overreach is often rebranded as legitimacy in the use of power.

Presidents depend on Congress far more than members of Congress appear to remember. Without statutory authorization, a president can accomplish little that endures. Executive-driven policymaking is inherently unstable, subject to reversal by the next administration. Durable national policy requires legislation. Only Congress can provide it.

When Congress fails to act, the consequences are predictable: erosion of the separation of powers, loss of democratic accountability, and steady drift toward executive dominance. Over time, that drift begins to resemble authoritarian rule—not because the Constitution permits it, but because Congress refuses to enforce its own authority.

Courts play an important role in checking presidential excess, but judicial review is slow and often incomplete. Illegal executive actions frequently remain national policy for years while litigation proceeds. Worse still, courts often dismiss disputes over war, peace, and national emergencies as "political questions," returning them to the elected branches for resolution. In those moments, congressional silence is not neutrality—it is abdication.

Congressional anti-takeover defenses.

In corporate law, anti-takeover defenses exist to prevent hostile acquisitions that strip authority from a company's governing body. In constitutional terms, a hostile takeover occurs when a president effectively seizes legislative power by making national policy without congressional approval. Emergency declarations and executive orders may appear lawful on their face, but when abused, they function as tools of legislative displacement.

Congress is not powerless in the face of such tactics. Beyond its lawmaking authority, it possesses investigative powers, subpoena authority, contempt powers, the Congressional Review Act, and—most importantly—control over appropriations. Hearings and investigations expose abuse; funding restrictions halt it.

When the president acts without clear statutory authorization, Congress should not allow the action to persist indefinitely. As a matter of institutional self-respect, no questionable executive action should continue beyond sixty days without an explicit congressional response. That response need not always take the form of new legislation. A Concurrent Resolution can formally state Congress's position without requiring presidential approval. A Resolution of Disapproval, though subject to veto, forces the issue into the open and preserves Congress's right to override a president's veto.

The objective is not merely to defeat the president in every dispute. It is to reaffirm a constitutional truth too often forgotten: ***Congress makes the law. The president executes it.*** Even when Congress loses a particular confrontation, it wins something far more important by acting—its legitimacy as a co-equal branch and Guardian of the Republic.

The power of the purse: Congress's most effective check.

The Constitution places control of the federal purse entirely in congressional hands. No dollar may be spent without congressional authorization. This authority is Congress's most potent—and most neglected—check on an imperial presidency. When Congress refuses to fund unauthorized executive action, the executive has no lawful means to continue it.

Yet members of both parties routinely shrink from using this power. Fear of government shutdowns, hostile media coverage, and presidential retaliation has persuaded Congress to treat the power of the purse as a nuclear option rather than a routine instrument of constitutional governance. History proves otherwise. Congress ended American involvement in the Vietnam War not through speeches or litigation, but by cutting off funding.

One House can close the purse.

A single chamber of Congress can stop executive overreach by refusing to appropriate funds. The Constitution could not be clearer: *"No Money shall be drawn from the Treasury, but in Consequence of Appropriations made by Law."* Spending requires affirmative action by both Houses and the President. Doing nothing requires only one House refusing to spend.

Neither the President nor the Supreme Court can compel Congress to appropriate money. One chamber may reject budget proposals, deny funding for specific programs, or condition expenditures on statutory limits the president opposes. This is not obstruction; it is constitutional design. The power of the purse ensures that executive ambition remains subordinate to legislative consent.

Refusing to raise revenue or debt.

All revenue bills must originate in the House of Representatives. If a majority of the House opposes the president's expansion of government, it can refuse to raise the funds necessary to support it. Without revenue, presidential ambition collapses into rhetoric.

The same logic applies to the debt ceiling. Created in 1917 as a borrowing restraint, the debt ceiling has since been raised repeatedly—more than seventy times since 1960—as federal debt climbed from under $300 billion to over $38 trillion. What began as a constraint on spending has become a mechanism for ratifying past excesses.

Refusing to raise the debt ceiling carries risk and should never be done casually. But it remains a legitimate anti-takeover defense. When used responsibly, it forces negotiation, transparency, and fiscal discipline. It reminds presidents that Congress controls the nation's credit card.

Legislative Riders are lawful constraints.

Congress can also attach conditions such as legislative

riders to appropriations and other must-pass bills. These riders direct or limit executive action and must be obeyed as law. Because appropriations bills are essential to government operations, presidents must either accept the rider or veto the entire measure.

Properly drafted riders are not legislative tricks; they are constitutional tools. They serve as Congress's counterpart to corporate "poison pills." Riders prevent unilateral executive policymaking by embedding legislative conditions into indispensable funding measures. Used judiciously, riders reaffirm Congress's authority to set policy boundaries.

Ending the culture of deference.

The real barrier to congressional oversight is not lack of authority, but lack of will. Over time, Congress has internalized a culture of deference to the presidency. Party loyalty, media pressure, and campaign finance dependency encourage members to serve presidents rather than the Constitution.

Reversing this trend requires members to recommit to their fiduciary duty to the institution of Congress. Structural reforms can help—bipartisan oversight resolutions, public review of executive actions, budgetary consequences for agency noncompliance—but no procedural reform can replace moral courage. The willingness to say no to a president of one's own party remains the clearest test of legislative integrity.

The citizens' role in restoring balance.

Citizens hold the ultimate lever of reform: their vote. Every two years, they can replace the entire House of Representatives. This power allows voters to change the course of government before executive overreach becomes entrenched.

By electing a House committed to fiscal responsibility and constitutional restraint, citizens can trigger a peaceful, lawful reset of federal power. One House, using the power of the purse, can restrain executive excess without Senate concurrence or presidential approval. If Americans want accountability, they must elect representatives willing to use constitutional tools in service of the people rather than political elites.

The people's legal revolution.

The separation of powers endures only if Congress and the electorate insist upon it. The Founders designed Congress to be the people's instrument of control, not the president's accomplice. By reclaiming the purse and enforcing oversight, Congress can restore that design. By electing representatives faithful to their fiduciary duty, citizens can again make government their servant—not their master.

The next chapter sets forth the essential commitments every member of Congress, and every candidate seeking office must pledge to honor if they intend to serve as true Guardians of the Republic.

CHAPTER 18

A CANDIDATE'S FIDUCIARY PLEDGE TO PRESERVE THE REPUBLIC

I seek office not as a partisan agent, but to serve as a trustee of the Constitution and a fiduciary of the institution of Congress. If elected, I acknowledge that I will always defend the Constitution's structure of separation of powers that safeguards the liberty of the American people.

ccordingly, I voluntarily pledge the following commitments:

1. **To Guard the Republic.**
   I will uphold, without compromise, the Constitution's separation of powers. I will actively resist the concentration of authority in any branch of government, including the presidency, and will not remain silent in the face of executive overreach.
2. **To Honor My Oath.**
   I will give undivided loyalty to the Constitution and to Congress as an institution. I will not subordinate

that duty to any president, political party, donor, or special interest.

3. **To Govern with Prudence.**
   I will work to restrain federal spending, confront the national debt, and limit borrowing to genuine public purposes that serve long-term national interests. I recognize that fiscal irresponsibility is a breach of trust with future generations.
4. **To Preserve Limited Government.**
   I will defend the principle that power should reside as close to the people as possible. I will support the repeal of obsolete or excessive federal laws and oppose the expansion of federal authority without clear constitutional and statutory justification.
5. **To Renew Representation.**
   I will voluntarily limit my service to no more than four terms in the House of Representatives and two terms in the Senate. I believe regular renewal of representation strengthens accountability and prevents the consolidation of political power.

I make this pledge freely, understanding that self-government endures only if those entrusted with power exercise restraint, courage, and fidelity to the Constitution.

Signed: ____________________________
Candidate for Congress

Date: ______________________________

PART V
CONGRESS MUST WRITE THE ENDING

CHAPTER 19

THE GHOST OF POLITICS YET TO COME IS STILL IN THE ROOM

The tragedy is that Congress still possesses, on paper, all the power it needs to be the greatest governing institution on earth.

The "Ghost of Politics Yet to Come," introduced in Part I, still haunts the American Republic. Before it can complete its grim task and bury the Republic, "We, the people" must act—either to change the conduct of Congress or to change Congress itself.

That change begins with truth. Members of Congress must admit that they have turned their backs on the Constitution by abandoning loyalty to their own institution and forsaking the defense of the separation of powers. The two parties have transformed what was once the world's greatest deliberative body into a perpetual, weaponized campaign machine. Debate has been replaced by tribal combat. Consensus has been sacrificed for raw power. Congress no longer legislates for the people; it performs for the cameras. Fear of the president's wrath has replaced courage. Its only remaining value is as political theater—packaged for media consumption.

The tragedy is that Congress still possesses, on paper, all the power it needs to be the greatest governing institution on earth again. If its members had the will to preserve the Republic, they could reclaim their authority tomorrow and confront the nation's most significant challenges. Instead, they cling to the status quo—power without accountability, position without responsibility.

Even within the legislative chambers, power has been ceded. Most members now serve as spectators to their own institution, deferring to a handful of leaders who script legislation behind closed doors and force votes before rank-and-file members can read the text. Committee chairs, once titans who forged landmark laws on civil rights, the environment, and banking, now shuffle along like obedient sheep.

Yet history teaches that decay need not be destiny. When institutions lose their purpose, renewal often arises from outside their walls. The question is whether Congress or citizens will once again summon the courage to be Guardians of the Republic.

As Post-2029 America strains under massive debts and endless wars, the people hope for a luminary to step forward. None does. The privileged enjoy their comfort too much to challenge the system that sustains them. Then one individual, Joe Nobody, decides to act.

Joe lives in a congressional district in North Dakota. Sometime after 2029, he launches a long-shot campaign against a wealthy, ineffective incumbent who has represented the district for decades. Relying on friends, social media, a knack for local press, and plenty of sneaker power, he promises that if elected, he will serve as a fiduciary to the institution of Congress, a trustee of the Constitution, and a defender of the separation of powers. He promises to take on executive overreach. His campaign theme is simple, yet profound: *Preserve the Republic*.

As part of his campaign, Joe challenges citizens across the country to run for Congress on the same pledge. He knows his odds are long, but he understands the power of a unifying message. A few weeks into his campaign, other Joe and Sarah Nobodys in Oregon and California pick up the banner. Within months, there are over thirty *Preserve the Republic* campaigns. All are grassroots campaigns powered by social media and faith in civic renewal. When the national press gives attention to the campaigns, the movement explodes. Soon, more than 100 districts will have candidates running under the same idea. Some even raise more money than they can spend. As momentum builds, several long-serving incumbents announce they will not seek reelection. A dozen more quietly prepare to retire. For the first time in decades, Congress feels the tremor of accountability.

A local reporter in New Mexico reflects on the phenomenon:

> *The campaigns seem propelled either by an invisible hand or by divine intervention. The "invisible hand," as Adam Smith described it, shows how individuals pursuing their own interests can, unintentionally, advance the good of society. Order and efficiency can arise organically, without a central authority directing every outcome. In this sense, the Preserve the Republic movement may not be the product of any one organizer but the natural convergence of citizens whose personal motives align with the collective interest of safeguarding constitutional order.*

In Joe Nobody's case, self-interest, and civic virtue merge. He wanted to defeat a useless incumbent and restore dignity to public service. His "product" was a campaign to

Preserve the Republic. Others saw its worth and joined in. By pursuing his own purpose, Joe Nobody inspired a national movement.

History supports the possibility of such an awakening. Political upsets often begin with an unknown who connects authentically with voters:

- **Senator Patty Murray**, the "Mom in Tennis Shoes," turned a dismissive remark into her political identity and won a U.S. Senate seat in 1992.
- **Senator Lawton Chiles**, an obscure Florida legislator, walked the state in cowboy boots, meeting citizens face-to-face and winning a Senate seat with 54% of the vote.
- **Governor Robert Graham** worked 95 different jobs to understand the lives of ordinary Floridians, building an unshakable bond with voters.
- **The Tea Party candidates of 2010** ran independently on fiscal restraint and constitutional principles—129 ran, 60-won, temporarily reshaping Congress.
- **Others**—Paul Wellstone, William Proxmire, Jesse Ventura—each embodied authenticity, grassroots energy, and defiance of the establishment.

Whether guided by an invisible hand, divine intervention, or simple luck, Joe Nobody put forth an idea and a roadmap for citizens to take back their government. Whether he wins is not the essential question. What matters is that he offered an idea and proved that one voice, when joined by others, can restore a nation's faith in its own capacity to act.

After the first wave of retirements, a surprising number of incumbents announced they would adopt the *Preserve the Republic* principles. Before the campaign season fully began, more than one hundred sitting members pledged to serve as fiduciaries to Congress and trustees of the Constitution. By election day, almost a majority of candidates—both challengers and incumbents—had committed themselves to those principles.

From her small desk in the New Mexico desert, the reporter wrote:

> *For the first time in living memory, the United States may be on the verge of electing a Congress that serves as Guardian of the Republic rather than guardian of party and profit. What began with one man and one phrase—Joe Nobody and his call to "Preserve the Republic"—has become a groundswell of ordinary citizens rediscovering their extraordinary inheritance. The story unfolding across the country is more than a legal revolution; it is a resurrection of the Republic.*

A few weeks later, the reporter filed another dispatch:

> *It appears the invisible hand is preparing to perform a miracle. The Preserve the Republic movement is about to sweep many of those who stood silent as authoritarianism took root in office. What's astonishing is that this rebirth of representative government isn't led by a celebrity, a billionaire, or a president—it's driven by the nameless and the tireless, by citizens who still believe their vote is an act of faith in the Constitution itself.*
>
> *If the miracle holds, historians may one day trace it back to a moment in the northern plains, when a single man decided he'd had enough and ran for Congress on the most enduring truth:*

The Constitution is only as viable as those elected to govern.

POSTSCRIPT

The conflicts members of Congress face are not rooted in ideology, but in constitutional duty.

From her small desk in the New Mexico desert, the reporter watched the House of Representatives live on C-SPAN. She was tracking the first House floor appearance of freshman Congressman Joe Nobody—one of eighteen *Preserve the Republic* candidates who unexpectedly won seats in the recent election.

Only days after taking the oath, he rose to introduce himself—and his first bill, the *Devolution of Power Act.* As he approached the well to file the legislation, decorum evaporated. Boos, hisses, and muttered profanities rolled across the Chamber.

The Speaker slammed the gavel again and again before summoning the Sergeant at Arms to remove several members whose insults violated House Rules.

Joe stood firm. Once order returned, he reiterated his campaign promise: he would serve as a fiduciary to the institution of Congress and safeguard the separation of powers. The words triggered a fresh wave of derision by many believing him to be politically naïve. But he did not flinch. He insisted on using his two minutes.

The reporter's shorthand captured the speech:

Mr. Speaker:

The United States is $60 trillion in debt. The nation is on an untenable path. We are placing our children into what amounts to involuntary servitude to the federal government. For decades, Congress has added to the debt without making a single sustained effort to reduce it.

The dollar has lost value against every major currency. We have lost our status as the world's reserve currency. Interest rates on Treasuries have soared beyond what the nation can responsibly pay. We know that a default would risk economic collapse, political instability, and potentially civil conflict.

There is only one realistic structural endpoint: the devolution of domestic powers to the states. Devolution relieves Congress of funding and overseeing thousands of programs that distract from its core duties—national defense, a stable economy and currency, and robust international trade.

We cannot cut enough, tax enough, or borrow enough to sustain this system. The only remaining option is to shed responsibilities—and domestic programs are the most logical responsibilities to shed.

Devolution is drastic, yes, but it is the only plausible reform. The federal government cannot support itself, much less fifty states and territories and provide subsidies to most industries, health care, and education. Eliminating federal grants to states would immediately save over a trillion dollars a year. We can save another trillion and a half dollars a year by eliminating subsidies to industry, health care, education, and by refusing to fund unauthorized appropriations.

The benefits are many:
- *Power returns to the voters most affected by decisions.*
- *States are forced to prioritize spending.*
- *Federal bureaucracy and budgets shrink.*
- *Responsibility is shared across governments rather than concentrated in Washington.*

Most importantly, devolution becomes a pressure-release valve for a federal government collapsing under its own weight.

And it aligns with the Constitution. The Framers never envisioned a national government running local schools, housing assistance, Medicaid, workforce programs, or infrastructure minutiae—yet today, Washington manages all of them.

Devolution allows each level of government to fulfill its responsibilities without federal micromanagement. It unleashes experimentation. It encourages innovation tailored to local needs. And it restores fiscal discipline by placing accountability where it belongs.

With citizens and government working together, accountability becomes possible again. Government becomes workable again.

Thank you for your attention. God save America.

—Congressman Joe Nobody

The reaction was subdued. A few members walked out. Most remained seated. From the video feed, the reporter could see many lawmakers staring ahead, speechless—uncertain whether they were more surprised by the freshman's bluntness or by the unfamiliarity of hearing a genuinely new idea proposed on the House floor.

Three minutes after Joe left the well, several members were still staring ahead, silent.

From her desk, the reporter could almost hear *the Ghost of Politics Yet to Come* struggling for breath. After haunting the Capitol for generations, it had finally encountered something it feared—a challenge rooted not in ideology, but in constitutional duty.

She started a new article and typed her first sentence:

It must be unbearably hard for members of Congress to confront the truth: they are to serve as trustees of the Constitution; they owe their fiduciary duty of loyalty to the institution of Congress; and only by checking the excesses of the Chief Executive and the Judiciary can Congress again become the Guardian of the Republic.

About the Author

William L. Kovacs writes from experience, not theory. After decades inside Washington—as a Capitol Hill chief counsel, senior vice president at the U.S. Chamber of Commerce, chairman of a state environmental board, and partner in major D.C. law firms—he has witnessed firsthand how constitutional limits are bypassed, how Congress relinquishes its authority, and how executive power expands without consent. He has testified before Congress forty times and participated in hundreds of federal rulemakings.

Congress: An Irrelevant Institution or Guardian of the Republic concludes Kovacs' trilogy on federal reform. In it, he delivers a stark warning: the Republic cannot endure if Congress refuses to act as a fiduciary to its own constitutional powers. When lawmakers transfer their loyalty to presidents and political parties, they invite authoritarian rule by default. If Congress will not reclaim its constitutional role, Kovacs argues, the responsibility—and the risk—shifts to the citizens themselves.

His trilogy includes:

• *Reform the Kakistocracy*, which exposes how the federal government transformed itself from one of limited powers into an immense central authority—without a single constitutional amendment.

• *Devolution of Power*, which offers a detailed roadmap for reversing the federal government's vast accumulation of domestic authority by restoring governing functions to the states.

• *Congress: An Irrelevant Institution or Guardian of the Republic*, contends that only Congress—through its lawmaking and power of the purse—can restore accountable government. Whether it succeeds depends on whether lawmakers can summon the courage, integrity, and will to check executive and judicial overreach. If they fail, Kovacs outlines the constitutional options citizens may use to reform Congress itself.

Reform the Kakistocracy received the 2021 Independent Press Award for Social and Political Change. *Devolution of Power* was a finalist in the 18th Annual National Indie Excellence Awards and earned a five-star rating from Readers' Favorite.

Kovacs is also the 2019 recipient of the Albert Nelson Marquis Lifetime Achievement Award from Marquis Who's Who.

www.ingramcontent.com/pod-product-compliance
Lightning Source LLC
LaVergne TN
LVHW010917110826
845149LV00013B/2400

* 9 7 8 1 9 7 0 5 6 0 2 3 7 *